PERU TRAVELS

Darren Stevens

Also by Darren Stevens

India Travels

http:www.fast-print.net/bookshop

PERU TRAVELS

A catalogue record for this book is available from the British Library

ISBN 978-178456-598-5

First published 2018 by
FASTPRINT PUBLISHING
Peterborough, England.

INTRODUCTION

The Trip

For my first trip to South America I could have chosen any one of the twelve countries to visit but I selected Peru, primarily because of Machu Picchu, one of the Seven Wonders of the World. This trip would see me visit my fifth of the series, having previously travelled to Petra (Jordan), the Colosseum (Italy), the Taj Mahal (India) and several sections of the Great Wall of China. I still have Chichen Itza (Mexico) and Christ the Redeemer (Brazil) left to complete the set.

I decided from the outset that it would be best to organise the Machu Picchu element first; once that most important part was secured I would then have fixed dates to build around. I knew in order to reach the site I first had to traverse the Andean Mountains beginning at Cusco; research led me to discover there were three main options:

Option one: The luxurious 1920s Belmond Hiram Bingham train transports passengers from Cusco to Aguas Calientes in just a few hours. The train is reportedly similar in style to the world-famous Orient Express and combines local entertainment with fine dining and drinks. The package includes a ticket for the shuttle bus (for the final leg up the mountain to the Machu Picchu sanctuary), entry to the site and a short guided tour. Upon completion of the site visit there would be lunch served at the Belmond Sanctuary Lodge hotel (a five-star establishment adjacent to the site entrance), before returning to Cusco via the same route. In total the round trip would take a mere thirteen hours to complete. There were several other train companies offering transport only, with the guide and the various tickets having to be booked separately.

Option two: The more traditional hikes along the Inca trail would take between two and seven days to complete depending on the starting point. A guide would assist with the meals and a porter with the luggage; a trail permit and entry ticket would also be included. As this was a camping trip, with only the most basic of facilities available, it also promised the accompaniment of groups of unwashed youths. I would usually refer to this type of expedition as the Aussie/Kiwi option. Not that there is too much wrong with the antipodean approach; I would probably do the same if I were on their limited budget and timetable.

Option three: The Mountain Lodges of Peru offered a six-day trip over the mountains utilising their purpose-built lodges. Day seven would see the visit to the sanctuary for a morning tour, with an option to further explore Machu Picchu on day eight. The Salkantay trail was a much higher route than the more popular Inca trail and would be less busy (but more tiring) as a result. As well as the guides, the party would also include chefs, porters and a masseuse. But most intriguingly of all, for the first five days, the travel between the lodges would be by horse!

Although the train option appealed to me from a comfort and luxury point of view, I never really gave it serious consideration as it seemed far too brief and left little or no time for delays. Besides I had already formed the opinion, even at this early stage, that the journey over the mountains was almost as important as the final destination.

As for the camping, it ticked the boxes in terms of duration and challenge, but I marked that down as my plan B and desperately tried to find an alternative.

Fortunately, there was indeed one other choice available which appealed to me as soon as I discovered it. The lodge to lodge trek promised to provide enough of a challenge during the day (horse riding over the Andes no less), while still delivering the reward of some comfort at the end of it. There would be proper beds, a private bathroom with shower, good food; I could have a massage and hopefully there would be some refined company. If all that wasn't enough, the lodges also had a bar!

Not a hard decision to make then - option three it was to be.

I conducted all of my correspondence with the company by email, beginning in the summer of 2015. I was initially offered dates for the following May, but that was conditional on at least one other person signing up. Even though the rep was confident that wouldn't be an issue, I would still have to wait before my booking was confirmed. This of course meant I also had to delay making all my other arrangements; I couldn't even book the flight.

The delay was a problem for me as I do like to arrange my trips as far in advance as possible. This is partly because I like to be organised and partly because my short-term memory isn't what it used to be. I tend to find if I don't complete a transaction at the first attempt I sometimes forget to revisit it. My mind tricks me into believing it has been addressed because I 'remember' dealing with it; the fact that the matter was left incomplete is occasionally lost to me.

I kept patient for about three months before deciding to proceed with all the bookings (outside of the lodge to lodge element); I really could delay no longer. Beginning with the fixed start date in the Andes in mind, I worked backwards four or five days until I found a suitable flight. This would allow me some time in Lima and Cusco for sightseeing and the important acclimatisation period.

The booking for the transatlantic flights was incredibly lucky in terms of timing because in 1982 the Peruvian government had sided with the Argentinians, against the British, over the Falkland's conflict. As a result direct flights between Peru and the United Kingdom were withdrawn. They only decided to reinstate direct flights two weeks before my trip, some thirty-four years later! This meant I could now fly direct, without having to change in the Netherlands. I opted for a British Airways (standard) World Traveller ticket for the out-bound flight, but I upgraded to Club World (business class) for the return. I reasoned I would be tired and maybe a little saddle-sore on the long journey home. Additionally, it was because I couldn't face the prospect of having a crying, preschool child sitting behind me kicking the back of my seat for hours on end; on this matter I write from experience!

Knowing I was to arrive in Lima in the evening, I booked a budget hotel for my arrival night, as I would need little more than a bed. For day two I opted for a five-star, coastal hotel which I financially justified by adding the two hotel costs together and averaging them out. This would allow me some time for sightseeing, before setting off to Cusco. For my return to Lima (with the trek and Machu Picchu completed) I chose accommodation in another location for variation. All these hotels were based in the recommended Miraflores district.

The next decision I had to make concerned the Lima to Cusco transit. I had a straight choice between an internal flight and a luxury coach. As I dislike flying I opted for the coach despite it being scheduled to take a mind-numbing twenty-two hours! The London–Lima–London flights were unavoidable, in practical terms, but in this instance I did have a viable alternative. Besides, I thought it offered the opportunity of seeing more of the country by driving along the coastal road and up into the mountains.

For my two nights in Cusco I booked the hotel owned by the Mountain Lodges of Peru, mainly as it was centrally located, near the main square. As well as being recommended by them (!), it also had the convenience of being the venue for the lodge to lodge team briefing on the evening before our departure into the mountains. There I would meet the other members of the group and be able to ask last-minute questions of the guide. Hopefully I would have recovered from the jet lag by the time I arrived in Cusco, as I would then have altitude sickness to contend with.

As I was to return to Cusco after the trek, I also booked an additional night in the same hotel, where I would be reunited with my excess luggage. My allowance on the trail was limited to how much the mules were permitted to carry, so my main case and laptop would have to remain behind. The allowance was a mere 10kg, all of which had to be squeezed into a holdall loaned to me by the company.

With my travel and accommodation booked, I then turned my attention to finding things to do and exploring places of interest. For Lima, I thought I would start off with a cookery class, as that would offer a good introduction to the country's food and drink. I do like to cook when I am at home, particularly on a Sunday (my only day of the week off work). After the morning cookery lesson was completed I would then embark on an afternoon guided bus tour of the city. I have found, on previous trips, that this type of excursion often provides a very good overview of new places. Upon completion of the tour I may then apply my new-found knowledge of the city to select areas I would like to revisit. Unfortunately, on this occasion, my time in Lima was somewhat limited, so I would just have to make do with the highlights. For balance, the following morning would see me visit a museum which holds numerous examples of recovered Inca artefacts.

For my time in Cusco, I booked a guided tour of the Sacred Valley to continue my Inca education. This area was once at the heart of their empire and therefore a must-see on this trip. Before I arrived at Machu Picchu I wanted to learn something about the Incas and how they lived. I selected a group tour which is something I rarely do given the choice. I just had to hope the guide would keep to the schedule as I had to be back in time to ready myself for the aforementioned lodge to lodge briefing later that evening.

Once based back in Lima, I allowed for an excursion to fly over the Nazca Lines. This trip would involve an initial three to four hour drive south from Lima, before a one and a half hour flight over the lines in a small aeroplane. As they could only be seen properly from the air I had little choice other than to fly, despite my loathing of this form of transport. Assuming I survived, (there were reports of very poor safety records) I would then stop off for lunch, before facing another three to four hour drive back to Lima.

In January 2016, some five months after my initial enquiry, I finally received confirmation of my booking from the Mountain Lodges of Peru. I was also informed that they had received a lot of reservations from hikers, so I was to be the only one riding. I hadn't thought hiking and staying at the lodges to be an option; it certainly wasn't offered to me. To be fair though, I had enquired about a riding trip, so it was probably right to assume that was my preference. They did try to offer alternative dates, where riders had been confirmed, but I declined as I now had far too many booking commitments to start making changes.

Although I usually plan my trips well and in fine detail, on this occasion I inexplicably paid little regard to the most important part until seven weeks prior to my departure. I had arranged to spend five days of my Peru expedition on horseback, without any idea whatsoever about horsemanship. When I think back it seems ridiculous not to have considered this aspect, as both my and the horse's safety should have been foremost in my mind. I had even been pre-warned by the company that I would be trotting along dangerous, narrow, shingle-laden paths and galloping across wide-open plains. I was advised that moderate experience was expected, but no proof of ability was required. In order to rectify this unforgiveable oversight, I booked six one-hour lessons at my local riding school. I was accompanied in the lessons by my niece Emily, while my dad looked on from the relative comfort (and safety) of the viewing gallery.

With the planning complete I just had to give some consideration to my clothing and accessories. The Mountain Lodges of Peru had helpfully provided a list of items to consider for the lodge to lodge element, so that was a good starting point. I just had to ensure I had something for all locations and all occasions. The most challenging purchases were of course related to the horse-riding gear, as I hadn't any experience whatsoever in that area. A local shop assistant kitted me out with a helmet, gloves, short boots and chaps (calf protectors in lieu of long boots). Breeches (elasticated, tight-fitting trousers) I ordered off the internet, along with some long-sleeved thermal tops. In the end my riding gear wasn't very colour-coordinated, with blacks, blues and browns, which was mildly disappointing. But with these final preparations in place, I just had to await my day of departure.

I hope this preamble has whetted your appetite for the story to follow. The bulk of the text I have written with the help of prepared notes I scribbled down during the trip. This was of tremendous help as my memory isn't too good - have I mentioned that? Along with the many photos I took this enabled me to capture the spirit and mood of the days, as well as the linear sequence of events. For the trek over the mountains I have added the elevations in metres, which were indicators for the dreaded altitude sickness; the higher the number the worse I felt, in general terms. I have also included some prices in Peruvian currency in order to make sense of the value of items in the country, five soles (S/.5) equates to about one English pound.

Be advised though, that the following pages are a record of my trip and not a guidebook in the conventional sense. There are plenty of other books on the shelves, penned by experts who have laboured for years accumulating facts and figures about Peru. In a small way I have tapped into these resources myself, notably for the information regarding the history of the Incas. They had long since departed before my visit, so I needed some assistance! Details of the origins of all additional material are listed at the back of the book, my gratitude to all of the contributors.

CHAPTER ONE

My arrival in Lima

My evening arrival in the Peruvian capital presented me with the perfect opportunity to step out and sample the city's nightlife. Although a little tired after my twelve-and-a-half-hour flight, I was still quite positive about the evening ahead. While I didn't intend to wander too far from my hotel, I was sure that with a little effort I would find somewhere to eat, drink and be entertained. However, as the taxi left the airport, this early optimism soon turned to frustration and dismay. Lima's roads were gridlocked so badly it appeared my evening examination of the city might be from the car as we crawled along.

Generally speaking, I was expecting Peru to be an extension of Spain in the same way that Australia and the USA are extensions of England. There are of course numerous differences between all of these countries, but I am only speaking in general terms. I hoped the Peruvian differences would be discernible to me, as they were the most intriguing part of all. I knew very little about these people or their customs at this stage. I had heard of the Spanish conquest, the Inca trail leading to Machu Picchu and the Nazca Lines, but very little else. I was determined to do my best to experience as much of what Peru had to offer in the eighteen days I had ahead of me.

For tonight, and the following two days, I would be based in Miraflores, an area of the city often described by guidebook writers as 'tourist friendly'. This usually means the district is home to the best (most expensive) hotels, restaurants and bars; however, on this occasion they also found it necessary to mention the area's very good safety record. This may be reassuring to some, but to me that often means that trouble is not that far away. As an inquisitive tourist, with no experience of the city, it is easy to wander off the suggested path into the more dangerous areas without realising, until it is too late.

I remember one example in particular, during my first trip to New York; I was twenty-three years old at the time. One moment I was happily strolling around Manhattan surrounded by throngs of people, the next instant I had turned a corner and I was suddenly alone. I was alone that is, apart from the unsavoury looking characters watching from the doorways of seedy looking establishments. Despite an early retreat and showing no interest whatsoever in what lay beyond their doors, I was followed for several blocks by an African American who attempted to offer me all manner of dubious sounding 'treats'. As I was maintaining my distance and trying my best to ignore him, he angrily called me a racist and things were potentially going to turn ugly. Now back amongst the masses, I stopped in full view of passers-by and we had a brief conversation…at arm's length. Thankfully, my confession to a lack of money finally proved to be a stumbling block too far and we parted company on reasonably good terms. I think I may have even promised to return later, a vague appointment I had no intention of keeping.

Despite my brushes with these sorts of characters, I still find myself wondering about the hidden parts of cities, the places I am not supposed to know about. To truly understand and appreciate a place you have to spend some quality time in all areas, rather than just pass through the popular parts as a tourist. Regrettably though, integration with the local people isn't always possible, particularly if language and comparative wealth are an issue. As a result I tend to find that my, often all too brief, excursions end up as just snapshots of the city and for the most part through a camera lens, which feels like a missed opportunity. I hoped this trip would be a little different, but I suspected not, as I had such limited time in each location.

My fifty-minute journey from the airport concluded with my being deposited outside the Antara hotel. My early fears concerning the traffic had thankfully proved to be unfounded; once we had cleared the painfully slow traffic near the airport we then joined the coastal road and moved along well enough. From the outside the hotel looked very welcoming; the brightness of the internal lights shone through the glass-fronted façade, in sharp contrast to the dimly lit street. If I had just been passing the premises, I might have mistaken it for a restaurant, albeit not a very popular one, with only two patrons dining at that time.

The check-in was straight-forward and once upstairs I found my room to be extremely spacious and reasonably well furnished. My only complaint was that it was a little on the stuffy side, which wasn't a big concern as I didn't plan to spend much of my waking hours in my room tonight. It was all I could really expect given the relatively low cost; tomorrow I was to depart for pastures new and hopefully to a better-quality establishment.

After a wash and a stub of my toe (more of that later), I quickly changed and returned to reception. There I was presented with a free glass of Pisco sour as a welcome gift. This Peruvian national drink was high on my list of things to sample, but I hadn't expected to try it so soon after my arrival. The top half of the glass was filled with white foam made of beaten egg whites, which did little more than temporarily deprive me of the alcohol below. When I sampled the brandy/lemon juice mixture at the bottom I found it certainly lived up to its sour name, but disappointingly it was a bit too sour for my taste.

Both the Peruvians and the Chileans lay claim to creating this cocktail and I am not going to enter into the debate about which country created it first as that would be a chapter in itself. There are numerous differences between the two drinks which include the alcoholic strength, the use of lemons or limes, the addition of egg whites or not and the different ratios of ingredients. With all this in mind it seems ridiculous that both versions have the same name. This must have been a result of people copying the more popular whisky sour recipe and tweaking it by using Pisco brandy.

I do drink cocktails upon occasion so I am not averse to the preparation of fancy looking drinks, in general terms. But adding egg whites for the express purpose of creating a layer of foam on the top of the drink is just wrong. When it comes to the taste, I am not a great fan of adding lemon or lime juice to my drinks either. Gin and tonic needs a small piece of the fruit, but in liquid form these sour additives disguise the taste of the main ingredient a bit too much for my liking. Overall, this feels like a waste of good alcohol and the Peruvian national drink committee needs to sit down and have a rethink.

The hotel didn't have what I would describe as a bar, just a cabinet with a few bottles of spirits on top. Unsurprisingly then, it seemed that the majority of guests had made alternative arrangements for this evening. After dutifully finishing my drink I decided to follow their lead and look for somewhere with a bit more atmosphere. As I exited the main door I realised, in my haste to leave the hotel, I had left my map upstairs with my belongings. I could have gone back to retrieve it, but instead I tentatively plotted a circular route around the hotel. I wasn't overly concerned with the layout of the city tonight as my desire to explore was limited to finding a local bar. After two right-hand turns I came upon a multi-level brightly lit casino. Crossing the road, I entered through the main door and rode the escalator up to the second level.

At the bar I placed myself on a stool and sampled my first bottle of Cusquena, which I found surprisingly good for a lager. As half of it had been poured into a glass I was able to drink the amber liquid while continuing to view the details on the bottle. My eyes were immediately drawn to the upper half of the gold label as it contained a representation of Machu Picchu. A quite unnecessary reminder of why I was here in Peru, but I was intrigued by it all the same.

My trip to China had proved to be quite a physical affair, as I had hiked over several mountains utilising their great man-made walls. I now had a similar challenge ahead of me as I planned to cross the unforgiving mountains of this other continent. The difference on this occasion was the method of the transfer (riding instead of walking) and the fact the 'wonder' was not the means of passage, but the ultimate destination.

As I took my time emptying and refilling my glass I alternated between people watching and focussing on items closer to hand. A younger solo drinker would have no doubt buried their head into a mobile phone by now. It never occurred to me that I was missing out on this option, and for that I am glad. I have a deep-rooted dislike for these devices when used for this purpose. I use my mobile phone for communicating; I don't regard it as a toy. I would delete all the unnecessary apps if I only knew how. Beer bottle labels, beer mats and the contents of the shelves behind the bar all make better reading material for the experienced short-term time-waster; I suppose I am from a different generation.

The casino had a large open atrium running through its heart and was spread over a number of floors. From my vantage point I could see over the balcony to the floor below, all around my floor and some of the balcony area above. I spied all the usual trappings of slot machines, card tables, roulette wheels and garish bright lights. To my right a few people arrived to join their friends for dinner and drinks, but generally there were very few people around.

As I am not a gambler, casinos hold little interest for me. I had assumed it contained a bar otherwise I wouldn't have entered at all. I quickly formed the opinion that the lack of atmosphere made this a one-beer venue, so after twenty minutes I drank up and departed for pastures new. As I headed for the exit I began to wonder if I was staying in the wrong part of town. It was 21:00 on a Friday and the casino had as many staff as customers; I just had to hope the next establishment was more to my liking.

Once outside I resumed my circuit of the block until the hotel was once more in sight. There I came upon a beggar who spoke remarkably good English. I couldn't quite place the accent, but he certainly wasn't a native of Peru. He was shouldering a couple of beaten-up dark backpacks and had the dishevelled look of someone who had been sleeping rough for at least a few weeks. As I was in a good mood I gave him some money, which was received with relative indifference. I don't usually give money to beggars; I am by nature a little suspicious, wondering if they are genuinely in need. If the need was real and the money solved today's problem, then what about tomorrow, the next day and weeks after? Then I wonder what the money will be spent on - alcohol or drugs are usually high on the list. He wasn't at his best tonight so he could have been using both to pass the time; passing the time for different reasons to me admittedly.

Now back outside the hotel my attention turned to a sign directing potential customers across the road to the 'Jazz Zone' via a narrow alleyway. When I had initially set off from the hotel I had noticed the sign, but I thought there might be better prospects around the corner. Now that my options were disappearing fast I thought it warranted further investigation. Crossing the road, I had just entered the alleyway when I heard the sound of laughter and mass applause coming from one of the premises. I quickly bounded up the stairs only to find a local comedian closing his act. The young girl at the ticket booth gave me a rather puzzled look as I surveyed the room from the entrance.

Had I arrived a little earlier I would have paid to enter and taken a seat; despite my obvious issue with the Spanish language it might have proved interesting. The performer would have effectively become a mime artist, in my eyes. I would have watched the timing and delivery of his rhetoric, the gestures he made, the response from the audience; I might have even had another drink. But there was no point dwelling on what might have been. With no reason to stay I slowly walked back down the stairs, just ahead of the departing horde. I then continued my, now increasingly fruitless search for a decent place to drink or dine.

After a few minutes surveying the outside of several of the establishments I eventually settled for a quiet little bistro called La Vida Misma. Once inside I found a dark and rather gloomy place with well-worn wooden furniture and faded posters adorning the walls; rustic, I think would be the best way of describing it. But on a positive note a three-piece band was in the process of setting up their instruments for their evening performance. This looked as good as it was going to get for tonight so I found a table near the front, off to one side, and took a seat.

My placement was intentional as it enabled me to view the band, the door and all the people in the room. It was obvious I was a foreigner and if trouble was imminent I wanted to see it coming. Not that I had any reason to think in those terms at this stage, but it doesn't hurt to be prepared when travelling alone in a foreign city. With some help from the waitress, who spoke little English, I ordered a chicken breast steak, salad and fried sliced potatoes. Simple food was all I required tonight and while I had her attention I also ordered a beer having now added the word *Cusquena* to my limited, but slowly expanding Spanish vocabulary.

The language barrier was possibly going to be my biggest challenge on this trip, putting the physical aspect aside for a moment. I have often thought it would be a lot easier if the whole world just spoke the one language. If it helped persuade the people of the world to change I wouldn't have a problem if it was something completely new, although I think English would be a good starting point. It seems easy to learn (I had little trouble) and is already widely spoken in numerous countries, being the international business language. Other nations could still add some of their own distinctiveness to it; a large percentage of English words already have French origins, so they couldn't possibly object. And I bet the people of China, Japan and Korea would also welcome a change, as they have to learn two forms of their language. The letters westerners recognise are straight-forward enough, but the elaborate Han-character, picture type of language, must be difficult to master. There is also precedent for change; although Latin is the basis of a lot of the romantic languages, such as French, Spanish and Italian, it is now seldom used in its purest form; it has been replaced.

When the food arrived I found that, despite it being simply presented, it was surprisingly tasty, *kudos* (Greek word) to the chef. Given the *décor* (French word) I had formed an early opinion of what to expect and anticipated something far less agreeable. (Last one!) Forgive the following *clichés* (French word), but it just goes to show you 'shouldn't judge a book by its cover'. If this was a 'taste of things to come', then I was going to have a most enjoyable trip.

The band played a mixture of Spanish and English language easy-listening songs and was generally fine. I found the song 'The Long and Winding Road' particularly apt given my impending trek over the mountains. Early into the set more locals arrived for their late dinner; maybe they had attended the comedy show. They seemed to know the band members well as they either shouted the occasional request or engaged in some good-natured heckling. This bistro had a nice vibe to it. There was no drunkenness (I had only just arrived); it seemed family-friendly and although I was a stranger from another country I still felt comfortable sitting there among them.

My initial concerns had thankfully proved to be unjustified; I have been to many other places, even near my own home, where this wasn't the case.

After spending just a few hours out in the city it was soon time to head back to the hotel. The six-hour time difference was now proving to be a major strain. Although the local clocks were almost at 22:00, my mind and body were still running on English time and that was now approaching 04:00.

It was hard to form an opinion about Peru at this stage, but my first impressions were positive. In just a few hours I had tried their national drink, listened to some local musicians and sampled some of their food. Not a bad start, but I was now feeling incredibly tired. Tomorrow my trip would start in earnest, but for now I just needed a soft pillow and a few hours' sleep to recharge the batteries.

CHAPTER TWO

Exploring Lima

Early this morning, I selected what I believed to be the typical Peruvian breakfast option from the hotel buffet. I discovered, within brown clay pots, an unidentified meat which tasted like pork, thinly sliced and fried sweet potatoes, scrambled egg with various additives such as smoked paprika (another educated guess); on the side there were slices of raw red onion. This was a hearty meal to start the day, but I am not sure if I could manage this type of food every morning.

After breakfast I decided to take another stroll around the neighbourhood, only this time I would be armed with my map. I had no time to spare getting lost this morning as I had a 09:00 appointment back at the hotel. As I looked up at the sky I saw it was completely overcast, but bright white rather than dismal grey and it wasn't at all cold. Back home I would have described it as a neutral day in May, with neither the cold showers of April nor the warmth of June on the horizon.

It didn't take long for me to leave the hotel, supermarket and other commercial premises behind and find myself well into the heart of suburban Lima. What I initially discovered wasn't pretty to look at. There were high-rise flats, which looked rather grey and drab, and smaller homes with high railings around their entrances; most had no gardens to speak of. These cheaper domestic properties in the city centre are often unattractive, as developers spend little time or money on the cosmetic side before moving on to their next project.

By way of contrast, I soon came across a vibrant vegetable street market where the locals were engaging the vendors in conversations, seemingly whether they were making a purchase or not. These stalls no doubt played an important role in the community, in terms of providing both sustenance and the opportunity for gossip. The women would soon return to their homes to prepare wholesome, home-cooked food rather than emptying supermarket packets into their pots. By cooking with these fresh ingredients, they would be limiting the levels of salt and other additives in their diets. The meals would be healthier as a result, providing they considered the portion sizes and didn't add copious amounts of salt themselves.

Adjacent to the vegetable stalls was a park with a two metre-high, black, wrought-iron railing enclosing it. The boundary looked a bit excessive, considering what was held within. Peering through these imprisoning walls I spied a well-kept garden full of lush green grass, well-trimmed bushes and tidy plants; I think the majority were white and red roses. I also saw statues sited within which brought a sense of reverence to the space, so perhaps this was a memorial park. Regardless of its purpose it looked a nice place for visitors to sit and rest their weary legs, as well as providing a place for the locals to enjoy in lieu of their limited personal outdoor space. Once I had circled the park I decided it was time to head back towards more familiar surroundings.

Upon my return to the hotel I completed the checkout process and stowed my luggage in a room adjacent to the reception desk. I had been careful not to wander too far this morning as I had arranged to be picked up by a rep from Haku Tours. The company offered cookery lessons which I thought might be a good way to sample some Peruvian cuisine. If I enjoyed the dishes I helped to cook, then maybe I could peruse the restaurant menus with a better idea of what to order. Last night I was assisted by the waitress and some pictures in the menu, so I just went for something simple, something I recognised with little risk.

I selected this particular company as soon as I read they were a non-profit organisation that supported the poor in the community. Their charitable work provides jobs for the noticeably needy in the inner city and extends to the outskirts where the forgotten peoples of the shanty towns reside. I now wish I had travelled to Peru a little earlier and volunteered to join one of their projects; that would have been both an interesting and rewarding experience.

My rep, Nathaly, was late in arriving so I felt more comfortable about asking her for a small favour. As I had checked out and no longer resided at this address, I saw little point in returning. I reasoned that, if I took my luggage with me, the driver could drop me at my next hotel straight after the lesson. The distance was only a kilometre or so between the two hotels and it would save me the hassle of ordering a taxi as soon as I returned. Nathaly immediately agreed to my request with good grace, for which I was grateful. I managed to transfer my luggage to the car without any assistance from the hotel staff, not that they offered to help - it wasn't that type of establishment.

'Stephanie from Amsterdam' was waiting patiently in the back of the car as I climbed in. I learned that she worked in the pharmaceutical industry and this was to be her last day of a four-week tour of Bolivia and Peru. I think I know even less about Bolivia than I do about Peru. After coffee, jungle and drug cartels I can't think of anything else to speak about and so it's not a country I have ever thought of visiting.

The lesson began with a drive to a local market where we were met by the chef, David, and another paying guest, Rachel, from the Isle of Man. She worked in banking, travelling to South America on a regular basis for work. Commuting on a regular basis to foreign countries sounds very glamourous, but I think it would soon become tiresome. There would be little time for personal recreation and a highly disproportionate amount of time spent travelling. The dates would also be determined by others and that could cause issues with social and family life. With all things considered, and given the choice, I think I will leave this type of travel to others.

The market was like many others I had visited, but similar in particular to the one I toured in Beijing, China. It was bustling with people and the waist-height stalls were overflowing with all manner of colourful produce. I wondered about the turnover of these perishable foods as there must be huge surpluses. How much wastage must they endure before it is no longer economically viable to bring these goods to market in such quantities?

Shopping isn't near the top of my list of things to do in my spare time; in fact, now I think about it, it isn't even on my list. But David did his best to make things interesting by asking us to guess the names of some items and providing free samples of others. We learned that the Peruvians have over four thousand varieties of potato, which seemed impossible to imagine. So many colours, textures, sizes, shapes and flavours to experiment with. It made me wonder why they still have that variety; surely people had their personal favourites? If so, would this not lead to the decline of the less popular varieties? It must be a regional thing where each community insisted on sticking to their own particular selection.

Before David purchased a container of chicha morada we were each given some to taste. The drink was served chilled and made from purple corn infused with cinnamon, pineapple and cloves; it is a very popular drink in Peru. Once you get past its strange, colourful looks it has quite a pleasant and refreshing taste. Although I imagine it would stain clothes and table cloths quite badly, which would put me off drinking it on a regular basis. Not that I am a messy drinker you understand, but accidents do happen and I would find the spillage most annoying.

The inside of a granadilla fruit on the other hand looks disgusting and has the texture and appearance of wallpaper paste with pips inside, or maybe frogspawn would be a better description. It was an effort to sample even a small piece of the slimy goo and I will not be repeating the experience no matter what the health benefits are. Stephanie and Rachel were less fussy and even made appreciative comments, although I noted they didn't ask for a second helping.

Worse was to follow when we ventured into the meat section though, as we were then exposed to the inner workings of chickens. They were split open with their innards left intact, presumably to demonstrate their freshness to the more knowledgeable customers. Whatever the reason, I didn't appreciate the display at all as I am used to seeing meats all neatly packaged or served cooked on the plate. As we continued our walk, David made several purchases. In the basket I spotted trout, beef, garlic, tomatoes, chillies, herbs, several different types of potatoes (of course!) and a mixture of fruit. Fortunately, there was no sign of the dreaded granadilla!

After an hour it was time to head back to the car for the short drive to our kitchen, where the real work would begin. Upon our arrival I was surprised to find it set up in the back garden of a youth hostel. Haku Tours, being a charity, understandably had to keep their overheads low, so they set up this mutually beneficial arrangement. The hostel allowed them the use of their facilities and in return they received some cooked meals from this locally renowned chef. This was quite a clever idea and in keeping with the Inca philosophy of bartering and sharing which I will expand upon later.

The kitchen area was sited some twenty to thirty metres away from the main building, presumably for fire safety reasons. The area measured four metres by four metres and was largely defined by earthen coloured, floor tiles. At the back was an L-shaped open-fronted room with a counter, oven, sink and lower wooden cupboards. On the left was a four-ring gas hob sat atop a small stand-alone cabinet. A six-seater table adorned with a white tablecloth completed the rustic-looking set up. Once up close I could see that everything looked clean enough, which had been foremost in my mind upon our arrival.

With the contents of our bags emptied onto the table we had quite a spread laid out before us, particularly when it came to the potatoes. There were a multitude of colours, shapes and sizes: red, black, yellow and brown, some long and thin, as well as the more familiar roundish types.

Before we began the lesson we donned our white Haku Tours logoed aprons and tall white chef's hats. I was then given the honour of performing the first task; the chef obviously knew talent when he saw it. The instruction went something like this:

Chef: *"Take the potatoes."*

Student: *"Yes chef,"* I replied enthusiastically.

Chef: *"Now scrub off the dirt under the tap."*

Student: *"OK,"* I said. This was great!

Chef: *"Now put them in the pot."*

Hmm…No peeling, slicing or dicing then. I didn't even get to add any water. I was feeling a little overqualified at this stage!

For the next phase I did get a little more involved. I was asked to slice and dice some tomatoes before peeling and crushing some garlic with a pestle and mortar. Not overly complicated, but at least I was participating. I do enjoy cooking, partly because I like to eat good food, but also because it has a method to it. If I purchase the right ingredients, and follow the recipe, I should end up with a tasty dish.

As the preparation element neared its end Nathaly informed me of a temporary change of plan regarding my luggage. The driver had to change vehicles, so he had taken my cases out of the car and left them in reception (the common area of the hostel). I tried to hide my horror at this news, but with little success. I was being informed that my laptop was sitting unattended in the reception of a youth hostel! Sensing that all was not well, Nathaly helpfully suggested we bring the bags into the garden adjacent to our seats. I agreed to this arrangement as quickly as it was polite to respond and walked quickly to retrieve them. I still can't believe she left my things unattended to come and speak to me; I think she's a little too trusting.

With the preparation complete we then assembled the classic Peruvian cold starter dish – ceviche, which is basically raw fish infused with fresh lime juice. The citric acid in the lime reacts with the raw fish and 'cooks' it, changing its appearance from pinkish to a more appetising looking white colour. It is then accompanied by chopped chilli, garlic, red onion and whole corn nuts. The ingredients are mixed with the diced fish pieces and stirred for a few minutes to help the chemical reaction take place. Trout was a good choice for this dish as it is firm; a flaky fish such as cod would have easily turned to mush with all the stirring.

Taking my first bite I reasoned that the proportion of the ingredients, like with most recipes, was critical to the taste. An imbalance of lime juice, garlic or chilli would upset the delicate taste. This starter course was for lovers of sushi and similarly prepared foods; it tasted fresh and the flavours were well chosen to excite the palate. As I thoroughly enjoyed it I made a mental note to include it on my list of dishes to try in a local restaurant.

At this stage Nathaly informed us her family had Chinese ancestry, which was evident in her facial features without her having to confirm her lineage. She talked a little about her culture and how her ancestors travelled to Peru in the mid-19th century in search of a new life in the west. Today she feels accepted in the community and hasn't had any issues with racism or at least there were no issues she wished to share with the group.

My post-trip research led to me to discover that when the African slave trade (mostly) came to an end, in the early 19th century, it was soon replaced by an East Asian 'coolie' alternative [1]. This arrangement was urgently needed as there was a huge shortfall in manual labour once the African slaves were freed. Chinese, Japanese, Filipinos and others from that part of the world were all promised short-term contracts either working in the fields picking cotton or building railways; at the end of the agreed term they were then free to settle. The reality was somewhat different of course as contracts were not always honoured. It often took many years, even generations, for these new settlers to obtain the rights their indigenous counterparts took for granted. Family life was even harder as there were very few Asian women living amongst the coolies, leaving the men to set up home with the local women instead. This was the second major fusion of peoples in Peru; the Spanish and Inca conflict leading to the first.

For the main course Rachel and I had the remaining and best parts of the trout, prepared in a tomato, garlic and herb based sauce. The fish heads were left to stew away with a bay leaf or two in a separate pot creating a tasty stock. As the tomato-based sauce reduced I occasionally ladled some of the fish stock into the pot. This ensured there was a tasty, concentrated fish flavour to the tomato base. At home I would have used a stock cube, but as we had bought the fish whole it was no trouble to boil the offcuts.

Stephanie had chosen beef for her main course and the chef cooked a small piece on the stove to demonstrate the method. He got the oil so hot it caught fire, which was initially a little intimidating for the young lady. For our part the rest of us stood well back and watched the spectacle unfold from a safe distance. I had my camera ready in case she caught fire or anything else interesting happened. The purpose of using oil at that temperature was to sear the meat, while keeping the inside moist; a lower temperature would have a stewing effect and make the meat very chewy. Once cooked, the beef was served with rice infused with some purple chicha morada liquid (an experiment), some peppers, onions and a little soy sauce. This was a stir fry essentially, something the Peruvians have no doubt adopted from the East Asians.

Once the potatoes were cooked through we all sat down together and sampled our efforts. I thought the fish was particularly good, but I would have added a little chilli to the tomato sauce. The potatoes had crispy skins and soft, fluffy middles. The colours of their centres ranged from white to orange, which came as a surprise and the robust pot made for very simple cooking, which was something to remember. It was a modest meal, but full of flavour, similar to last night's late dinner.

With the meal complete we then sampled some Pisco brandy with ginger ale, which I confess I much preferred to the Pisco sour cocktail version. I was a little disappointed to discover this, as I do hold the classics and other traditions in high regard.

Last of all we tried some coca leaves which are used primarily in Peru to fend off altitude sickness. Given that Lima is at sea level I assumed we were sampling from a novelty perspective. The leaves are the starting point for the production of cocaine, although a lot of chemicals and processing has to occur before that is produced. I found the leaves very bland in flavour and so a bit of a chore to chew. When I tried a bunch rolled up I did feel a numbness creeping down the back of my throat, similar to being at the dentist. I suspect this altitude sickness remedy is merely a numbing of the brain to alleviate the light-headedness/headache effects; these harmless looking leaves are essentially painkillers. I suppose in the times before tableted medication this was a necessary commodity. Today however, I would suggest using the tablets, as consumption of the leaves in any great quantity may do more harm than good.

After the lesson I was dropped off at the Miraflores Belmond hotel as requested. My first impressions were of a hotel that was certainly an upgrade on the previous establishment. Palm trees flanked the main multi-stepped entrance and the stand-alone structure rose high into the Peruvian sky, along with several others in the immediate area it should be said. This area looked like it was the most recent addition to the Lima project and this hotel one of its gems as it overlooked the nearby Pacific Ocean. As expected a porter took my large bag inside, while I finalised the course payment (S/.200), tipped Nathaly (S/.50) and said my goodbyes. It had been an interesting first half of the day with an early lunch and the bonus of transportation to my new hotel.

At reception I was advised that my room wouldn't be ready until 15:00, but instead of waiting the forty minutes in the lobby, I left my cases in their care and departed for my next excursion. The meeting point for the city bus tour was at the Larcomar shopping centre, which was only a ten-minute walk from the hotel. After receiving initial directions from the concierge, I found the shopping centre easily enough, but it took a little while to find the exact meeting point. I had a voucher to present to the bus tour reps, but they were nowhere to be seen. A security guard directed me down an escalator to the company's office, which felt like a rather unnecessary detour, but at least I then received accurate meeting point directions.

I find Viator an excellent company when it comes to suggesting itineraries and providing vouchers for tours in foreign cities, but the directions and details concerning the meeting points often leave a lot to be desired. It would be better if they were written by people who had little knowledge of the city, rather than by someone who assumes everyone knows the area as well as they do.

Once on board I headed upstairs to the top deck, towards the back and on the left, one of the few unoccupied seats left in fact. I hadn't expected the bus to be full, quite the opposite. I had thought, as I was joining at the recommended meeting point, that I would be entering an empty bus along with all the others in the queue. I just had time to take my seat before the bus pulled away. We were headed for the old part of the town, where we were to stop off and continue the tour on foot.

Halfway to our destination we stopped at Huaca Pucllana for a photo opportunity from the bus. The site may be described as a series of walled areas with a flat-topped pyramid at its heart. The site had a ceremonial heritage over a thousand years earlier; its creation pre-dated the Incas. From my viewpoint I could just make out the small clay bricks in the walls which separated the various areas. It wasn't a visually striking monument, but then I don't believe it was meant to be. I wasn't to know at the time but towards the end of the trip, upon my unexpected early return to Lima, I would be paying a visit and seeing it up close.

After an hour we reached the main square, Plaza de Armas de Lima, at the heart of the old town. Upon our arrival we disembarked and our guide then gave us a well-practised speech about the location. The name translated directly as 'Parade Ground' and was built by the Spanish conquistadores in 1535. The square is the oldest public space in the city and is surrounded by the most important buildings, including the cathedral and the Government Palace (Palacio de Gobierno).

The surrounding buildings were all primarily yellow in colour, with white trim around the windows. Some had huge black wooden balconies suspended outside the windows. They were apparently of Moorish design; the Arabic peoples had influenced the Spanish builders (back home in Spain) many years earlier. The contrast in colour was striking and the construction made them appear to hang in mid-air. Despite their ornate design and practical application they looked like barnacles on the faces of the buildings, a real eyesore.

At the centre of the square was a large, multi-tiered, black fountain capped by a trumpet-playing character standing on one leg. The fountain was made of bronze and looked a worthy centrepiece; the proportions and design were very much in keeping with the surroundings. The original fountain was commissioned by Francisco de Toledo and completed in the late 1570s, but it was replaced by the one I saw before me by Garcia Sarmiento de Sotomayor in the early 1650s. Presumably the new Governor liked this design better or more likely he just wanted to make his mark on the square.

After the talk we had a token fifteen minutes' free time to explore the area for ourselves, which was not really enough time to do anything but walk around and take a few snapshots of the immediate area. This goes back to my earlier point about viewing a city through a camera lens; it would have been good to visit each of the buildings and go inside, if that were possible.

After the tour of the square was complete we departed on foot for the Basílica y Convento de San Francisco de Lima which took six or seven minutes to reach. Inside, I was surprised to find a wedding ceremony taking place; I didn't know what to make of that, a private moment being shared with the public. I also don't know why I bothered to go inside at all as it looked exactly the same as every other church or cathedral I have visited. I don't know what I expected to find on this occasion; I suppose it was just the curiosity factor.

When we regrouped the guide led us to a large empty room that had once served as a dining area. At the far end there was a large painting on the wall depicting the legendary Last Supper scene. I don't think I need to elaborate too much on whose last supper it was, but just in case you didn't know it was a man named Jesus, a soothsayer or the son of God depending on your beliefs. This painting was a little different to any other that I have seen though, as the table's centrepiece hosted a cooked guinea pig. This Peruvian delicacy is still enjoyed today and I would have the opportunity to sample a cuy, as they call it in these parts, when I reach the mountain lodges. Something to look forward to!

The artist had put his own twist on this biblical event, either to demonstrate a sense of humour or more likely to annoy the Catholic invaders. Whatever the reason, this is the thing with paintings; they aren't photographs, they are just an artist's impression of an occasion, an opinion.

The most famous depiction of the event was painted by Leonardo Da Vinci in the late 15th century. There is some debate regarding the participants, forming yet another conspiracy theory. There are persons who insist that the individual to the left of Jesus (as we look) is Mary Magdalene, and not John, who was often portrayed in an effeminate way in paintings. That conveniently brings a lover into the story and the possibility of a bloodline. People create these types of stories to suit their own agendas and then they try to convince others by using a PAINTING, created hundreds of years after the event, to back up their ridiculous theories. The truth is lost forever, as the church has made so many changes to the Bible to suit their needs. The facts, if I may call them that in this context, have been lost long ago. I haven't read the Bible, but I understand that these days there are fewer stories concerning dragons within the text.

The most interesting part of this tour was yet to come. As we exited the cathedral we turned to our right and accessed the catacombs via an adjacent entrance. This was quite a macabre dish to serve up to tourists, but a fascinating prospect all the same. Upon entering we soon found ourselves in a labyrinth of mazy passages, with large groups of people in front of us and another crowd behind. This was certainly a popular place to visit, although not for the claustrophobic. The ceilings were low and the floor uneven, this meant I had to watch both my head and my step in equal measure as we advanced.

We soon learned that several hundred years ago the rich and gullible people of Lima thought they were securing themselves a safe passage to heaven by paying to be buried here. In reality, after a few years interred in the ground, their bodies were exhumed to allow room for more paying customers. But, rather than maintaining the integrity of the exhumed skeletons, their bones were sorted into different types and placed in boxes or open pits...and there were thousands of those.

The guide did his best to keep our group (and the one ahead) moving and his interventions were needed as people were often stopping to view the contents of the pits as they were passing. I could now taste the ancient dust in the air as we ventured along the tight passages. The low light levels also helped to maintain a morbid and reverent atmosphere, but nothing was to prepare us for the last spectacle set before us. In a very large pit human skulls had been arranged in a vast circular pattern. I struggled to fathom the reasoning behind this exhibition. It was bad enough that this religious organisation had disgracefully desecrated the dead for financial gain, but to then sort their heads into such an 'artistic' display was beyond shame.

After the catacomb tour was completed I caught the tour bus back to the shopping centre, arriving back at 18:15 and I was back at my hotel not long afterward. There I collected my things from reception and retired to my room for a break. I didn't bother unpacking as I was to depart the next day.

By 21:00 I was seated in the bar area sampling some more Pisco (with ginger ale), just for research purposes. For my evening meal I just ordered a club sandwich, but despite my best intentions I left half the food and some of my second drink as I was feeling extremely tired and even a little dizzy. I don't recall experiencing jet lag on any of my previous holidays, but here it was affecting me quite badly during these first few days. At times I was so tired I felt a little drunk, and not in a pleasant way.

Tomorrow I had the altitude sickness problem to contend with, which would be another new and unpleasant experience. It usually occurs above 3,000m, so it was not an issue at all in Lima, which sits at a lowly 1,500m. However, the journey through the mountains to Cusco would see this gradually rise to 3,400m, where my problems would begin. Before I left the bar for the evening I asked the waitress for some tips regarding the condition. She recommended that I should only eat soup and fish as they are easy to digest. It seemed that diet is important as the body has trouble functioning normally in the rarefied air.

Hopefully then, my early night would rid me of this awful tiredness, because the next malady was expected to be even worse.

CHAPTER THREE

Departure from Lima

Given my tiredness, the last thing I needed was to start the day by being woken at 06:00 by my hotel alarm clock. I did wonder if this was a ploy by the hotel staff to encourage guests to leave their rooms early on their day of departure. I suppose it could have been set by a previous guest, but a knock on the door by the maid at 08:15 only strengthened my belief that it was intentional to get me moving. As I was already wide awake I kept my sense of humour and asked her to come back to service the room in an hour.

I planned to use my last few hours in Lima visiting the Larco Museum, which contains a large collection of Inca artefacts. These items were originally part of a private collection, which have since been made available to the public. I am often in two minds about visiting museums where relics from the past are on display. Admittedly I am curious to see how people in previous eras lived, but at the same time I am also of the view that archaeologists are grave robbers in the main. They often know they are digging where bodies are laid to rest, but they continue onward regardless as they believe the dead may be bearing gifts. They should accept that these people were buried because their loved ones and their society did not want them disturbed. If this were not the case, if it were of little importance to them, then they would have been left on the surface. I accept this view may be tinged with a little hypocrisy given my own curiosity, but that is how I feel and why I am often in two minds about visits of this nature. Incidentally, when members of the Indian Parsi religion die, they aren't buried; instead they are left in a designated high point for vultures to gorge upon.

When I made enquiries about transport, the hotel offered me a choice between a hotel car for S/.100 and a local taxi for S/.18. I unsurprisingly chose the latter and took note of the company's telephone number for the return journey. The disparity in cost between the two companies did not come as a complete surprise to me, as the larger hotels tend to offer these types of services for a higher price in exchange for a good quality vehicle, driven by a trusted and known individual. We as customers are then supposed to feel comforted in the knowledge that they have considered our well-being to be of the upmost importance. From experience I have found there is usually nothing to choose between the two options, apart from the price.

The taxi arrived later than expected due to a half-marathon road race crossing in front of the carpark entrance. I thought this was going to cause a long delay for our departure as well, but thankfully the officials used their judgement to let us through when a suitable gap appeared. We continued being hampered in this fashion for a few kilometres until the driver had the good sense to turn around and try an alternative route. These short delays meant I was now half an hour behind my self-imposed schedule, arriving at the museum at 09:30.

As I exited the taxi I was pleased to discover the museum was set in the grounds of a wonderful garden, which made for a pleasant beginning to the visit. Most of these types of exhibition centres are just nondescript buildings with nothing else on the exterior to inspire the visitor.

The floor surrounding the structure comprised a sea of red herringbone style paving, with potted plants helping to break up the vast expanse of colour. The main building and retaining walls were whitewashed in that Mediterranean way, reflecting the morning sunlight. The tall and colourful surrounding bushes helped to mask the neighbouring buildings, giving the impression that the museum was set in a rural location instead of the suburban backstreets of downtown Lima.

As I paid the entrance fee of S/.20 I took the opportunity to ask the receptionist if I could use her telephone to call a taxi when I was ready to depart. I thought this was a simple enough request, but it took a while for my wish to be understood and granted. I could sense she was wondering why I wanted a taxi so soon after arriving. It took me several minutes, repeating my request with gestures, before I eventually got the message through. The museum had only been open half an hour so I pretty much had the place to myself as I set off to explore the exhibits.

From the reception I turned left and entered the first gallery where I found display cases full of unusual, glazed clay pots – most depicting human or animal forms with spouts exiting from either their heads or their bodies. They were similar to Toby jugs in design, but a little less refined in the detail. The human types didn't appear to be depicting actual people as the facial features were too imprecise. They also weren't as colourful as they could have been, just differing shades of brown; maybe the colour had faded over time, I couldn't be sure. One thing that impressed me immediately though was their condition as they looked as if they had been formed the day before my visit. The owner must have been really selective in his choice of what to buy and what to put on display. It was hard to believe that these artefacts had survived for five hundred years without so much as a scratch.

The next gallery contained modern-day mannequins adorned with decorative gold plates about the upper part of their bodies. The plates were clearly not armour as they were too thin to offer any real protection. These golden costumes must have been for ceremonial use and would have sparkled in the sunlight, although at the same time they did look quite primitive. Some of the mannequins also displayed headwear made of overlapping coins, in a fish scale pattern. These did not appear to be crowns exactly; they were more like lofty headpieces, in differing states of repair.

I found the last gallery in this section set up more like a storeroom than a formal display. There were rows of blue open racks each filled from floor to ceiling with human-head jugs. In adjacent racks there were also reproductions of birds perching on walls. All the birds looked like puffins, which probably meant there was an abundance of these creatures at the time of the Incas. I got the impression that the collector had opened up his prize specimens to the public, while still being undecided about what to do with the rest of the collection. I suppose as these items were numerous, but very similar in design, it would have been difficult to have them all spread out in glass cases. They would have taken up a lot more space and the overall design of the exhibition might have been compromised.

In order to visit the final gallery, I had to exit the main building and walk along a signposted winding path. This area was kept separate because it contained an exhibition of erotic pottery. I found the shelves full of the same types of pots as before, only this time there were two combined figures to each pot. Each depicted male and female figures in Kama Sutra poses, sitting, standing, kneeling before each other. These must have been used as fertility symbols, maybe taking pride of place in homes in the hope that the families continued their succession lines.

Once I had completed the tour I took a slow walk through the surrounding gardens, until I came across the dining area. As I was ready for a short break I took a seat and browsed through the menu. It took me quite a while to choose some suitable Peruvian dishes only to be told at the counter that they weren't available. In the end I had to settle for burger and chips which was extremely disappointing (choice-wise) to say the least. I think the staff had taken it upon themselves to limit the options on the menu as it was Sunday and still relatively early. I did sort of make up for it by selecting a Pisco drink with coca leaves blended in, served of course with the obligatory frothy top – a bit early for alcohol and drugs I know, but I only had the one. Once I was satisfactorily rested, I paid the bill of S/.60 and headed back to the main entrance.

At reception I booked my return taxi and immediately headed down the ramp to the nearby gift shop, sited adjacent to the exit. There must have been a taxi rank nearby because I was called to the main gate before I had even entered the shop. I was still determined to make a souvenir purchase though, so I kept him waiting a few minutes while I quickly browsed the shelves. Once underway I thumbed through the pages of the large book I had purchased. It contained pictures of all the exhibits I had just viewed, which was just as well, as I had my doubts about the photos I had taken. The rooms were a little dark and the much-needed camera flashes often ruin photos as they reflect off the glass cases.

The museum wasn't quite what I had expected it to be; for one thing it seemed a lot smaller than my recollections of the pictures on the website. Looking back though, I think I must have mixed up the Museo Larco with the Museo Oro del Peru. The latter holds a very large collection of gold artefacts and weapons from all around the world. It would have been good to visit both, but during my preparations I must have opted for the dedicated Inca option; understandable given the nature of this trip. Still, I had no regrets about my choice; it was certainly a place worth visiting.

Upon my return to the hotel I spent half an hour updating my notes, recharging my various appliances and downloading the photos onto my laptop. I wasn't pestered any further about leaving my room, but shortly before midday I dutifully reported to reception to check out. While at the reception desk I booked another taxi and spent the ten minutes waiting time in the pleasant lounge area relaxing until it arrived.

In some ways I wished I could have spent more time at this hotel as it was very comfortable and set in lovely surroundings. With hindsight, I could have allowed an extra day in order to chill out and relax. I could have spent the time constructively, drinking Pisco before having an afternoon siesta, all to help with my acclimatisation of course. Excursions and other activities are interesting and a must for these types of trips, but they are also both mentally and physically tiring.

My very long journey to Cusco began with the relatively short taxi ride to the Cruz del Sur coach station. We had no issues exiting the carpark as the earlier road race had long since been completed. I arrived just before 12:20, having only taken fifteen minutes to complete the journey. I was nearly two hours early, but at the time I had no way of knowing exactly how long the check-in process was going to take.

Several months earlier I had booked what was described by the company as a 'luxury coach' to take me from Lima to Cusco. This was mainly due to my dislike of flying, but I also reasoned that I might get to see more of the country from the ground; I was here for a sightseeing trip after all. Unfortunately though, this meant I now had a twenty-two-hour journey ahead of me, instead of the more reasonable two-hour flight.

The coach station was very busy and I was advised by a passing station worker to first present my documents to the person at the tourist information desk. From there I was directed to the one of the counters on the main desk where the attendant spoke English. Once my details were confirmed, and a receipt stapled to my voucher, I headed off to a third location to check-in my luggage.

As I queued I read a sign informing me that my luggage would be checked for both its size and weight. As the limit was only 20kg I immediately knew that was going to be a problem. At the airport my case was already very near the maximum limit of 25kg and that was before I had purchased my souvenirs. When I looked around at the other passengers' belongings, it also stood out in terms of size, when compared to the plethora of rucksacks and holdalls. But at least I only had the one item to check-in; I just had to hope the attendant would be of the same opinion.

As I gradually edged forward my anxiety began to rise and I began to consider all the possible options open to both me and the staff. Paying an excess fee wasn't a problem as it would no doubt be a token gesture. What I really didn't want to do was remove items from my case and carry them separately – that would be a real pain as I already had my laptop to manage. But that would only take care of the weight issue; what if they complained about the size? I couldn't exactly hack a piece off the side of the case. Step by step I drew nearer to the counter fearing the worst.

When my turn arrived I intentionally avoided eye contact with the attendant as I helped him lift my very large case onto the counter. After he took sole control it dropped heavily to the floor on his side of the counter with a dull thud; he then struggled to haul it over to the scales while I waited with bated breath. I stood anxiously watching as he viewed the readout; it was indeed several kilograms over the prescribed limit. Then to my surprise he just turned around and presented me with a receipt without passing any comment whatsoever. There were no histrionics or dramas of any sort, no further action required. This is where countries like Peru have got it right. There are numerous places I have visited where an over-officious employee would have made a big issue out of this type of situation. I appreciate if everyone did it then there might have been a problem with overcapacity; after all there is only so much weight the coach can carry or fit in the hold. But, given that most of the other bags were small, this was hardly a big concern here.

I now had nothing to do for the next ninety minutes, other than wait for my departure, which added a big chunk of time to the already lengthy journey. I could have ventured up one level to the small cafeteria, but I had eaten at the hotel and dined again at the museum, so I wasn't at all hungry. Instead I took a seat opposite reception and read a magazine. I occasionally glanced up from my reading to view the digital clock opposite my position and ticked off the minutes as they slowly passed.

With half an hour to go I stood and walked over to the loosely forming queue that had begun to gather by the departure gate. Fifteen minutes later we were invited to step forward and enter the security scanner, which was positioned adjacent to the exit at gate four. Once my hand luggage and paperwork checks were completed I was allowed to enter the coach, where I quickly headed upstairs to find my new temporary home.

When I presented my ticket to the stewardess she helpfully directed me to a single blue leather seat at the very front and right-hand side of the aisle. If I could have selected a seat, I would have chosen this one; it was on its own with great views directly ahead via the large upper windscreen. The front and side window were framed by blue curtains which seemed to be the colour of choice throughout. As I only had a low bulkhead behind me, I could also recline my seat as much as I wanted without disturbing anyone; this allocation was no doubt an advantage of booking so far in advance.

We set off at precisely 14:00 which was promising for the journey to come; I couldn't even contemplate a delay of any kind at this early stage. As I glanced around at my fellow travellers I saw they were a mixed bunch. There was a small group of teenage French girls immediately to my left, lots of locals and the occasional western backpacking couple. Generally, they were people who either couldn't afford to fly or they were to depart the coach at stops along the way, well before we arrived at Cusco. During the daylight hours we would be driving along the southern coastal road, but as night descended we would head east up into the mountains. We would then be at the mercy of poorly lit mountainous roads all through the night. Hopefully the driver was experienced and knew the route as this really wasn't the sort of road trip where you could learn as you went along.

Not long before setting off I spied my first tuk-tuk. I had seen plenty of these in India and a few in China, but for some reason I hadn't expected to find them here in Peru. A tuk-tuk is essentially a three-wheeled motorbike with a shell around it. It is not very stable when turning corners, but it is cheap to run (due to the small engine size), making it truly the vehicle of the people.

The traffic was fairly light as we headed out of the city and the coach thankfully rode comfortably on the road. The other road users' skills were pleasingly similar to those in Europe rather than the Far East, so my initial concerns about safety were eased. I should feel safe on the roads wherever in the world I am, but there are some countries where the population deliberately ignores the rules of the road, if they even know them in the first place.

At 19:15, the stewardess presented us with our evening meal served atop a small blue tray. There were three rectangular, covered dishes which I soon discovered contained a cold bean salad, a hot main course of chicken with vegetables and lastly a soft bread roll. While the food was at least edible I made the mistake of accepting the offer of an Inca Kola drink. Prior to boarding the coach I had never heard of it, but trying it seemed a good idea at the time. It was something new, with a link to the country

I was visiting, so why wouldn't I? Once you get past its illuminous yellow appearance the taste is truly dreadful, particularly if it is served at room temperature, as in this case.

I understand that in terms of popularity the drink outsells Coca-Cola in Peru, while outside the country it is in fact partly owned by Coca-Cola and they widely distribute it around the world. It is said that the taste reminds people of a mixture of bubble gum and cream soda, but that does not tell the whole story and is being rather kind. It is loaded with caffeine and sugar, as most of these types of drinks are, but best of all some advertisers (desperate for some sort of USP) declare it has '*that highly valued yellow color*', which is not a view that I happen to share.

Post-trip I discovered a most shocking fact…it was actually invented by an Englishman, named Joseph Lindley! [2] After moving his family to Peru in the early 20th century he spent many years trying to perfect the taste. In 1935 he launched the Inca Kola brand to coincide with the anniversary of the foundation of Lima, four hundred years earlier. It could also be said that this marked the beginning of the Spanish conquest and the demise of the Incas, but that seems to have been overlooked, despite the irony of the name.

After the remnants of dinner were stowed away I soon discovered a serious flaw in my plan to see the sights of Peru from the ground. For the first six hours or so we were on the motorway which wasn't very interesting, apart from the ocean and sandy beach to my right. Then, with night fast approaching, the stewardess drew the curtains, plunging the interior of the cabin into semi-darkness. The view from my front row seat, with its wonderful sightlines, was now no better than any other on board; from a sightseeing perspective I might as well have been at high altitude in an aeroplane. We did have individual television screens to keep us amused, but mine was stuck stubbornly on a popular Spanish language channel and refused to budge.

The French girls were now starting to grate on my nerves with their inane chatter and scratchy, headphone-delivered music. All in all, with little to stimulate my brain and minor aggravations all around, I was mentally starting to feel the strain. We continued onward throughout the night, stopping every couple of hours to either drop off or pick up passengers and light cargo. Presumably, we also changed drivers, but it was hard to tell from my viewpoint even though I was nosily peering through the curtains. At 23:00 I made a genuine effort to settle down and get some sleep, but even with the thin blanket and fully reclined seat that proved to be impossible. After two hours I gave up and just closed my eyes, forcing myself into a semi-meditative state. I had little choice left but to mentally prepare myself for the most uncomfortable night of my life.

CHAPTER FOUR

Cusco

Although I sat up and opened my eyes at 05:00 I was pretty sure I hadn't slept at all last night. I now felt a little light-headed and nauseous, but I wasn't sure if that was from the higher altitude (only 2,300m at that point) or that truly dreadful Inca Kola. Whatever the cause, I knew I was going to need the medication as soon as we reached Cusco. Hopefully I would find a pharmacist who spoke English, otherwise I would have to ask the hotel receptionist to write down my requirements to pass along, which wouldn't be ideal.

The stewardess drew the curtains at 07:00 to reveal a quite dramatic change to the scenery. Yesterday it had been mostly motorways, admittedly with the sea view to break up the monotony of road after road; now this morning we were surrounded by mountains. When I looked down into a neighbouring valley I could see masses of low-lying clouds. At first it looked really strange to see the clouds both above and below; it is a common enough sight on an aeroplane, but here it seemed surreal. As we continued our steady climb towards Cusco I realised there was something lacking from the picture before me...signs of life. Despite the area's natural beauty this was a somewhat barren place; the river to my right generated the only movement for kilometres as it meandered alongside the road.

The stewardess served breakfast at 07:30, but I only picked at the items in my polystyrene dishes. I had been given a chicken salad roll, a cupcake and some peanuts, but I had little appetite for any of it. There was nothing wrong with the meals on board; I just wasn't in the mood, due to my not feeling too well. I also prefer to eat when I am hungry and not when someone decides to place food before me.

We soon approached a small town which reminded me a little of India, only without the masses of animals wandering around. It was hard to absorb the sight before me as there was so much going on. There were now multi-coloured tuk-tuks everywhere, each with the most artistic paintwork adorning them. The people that were not riding in tuk-tuks were cycling, walking or driving in large heavily laden vehicles. Groups of school children were making their way on foot to their nearest education centre. I wondered how long it took them to complete their journeys every day – there were no schools in sight.

The buildings, although square or rectangular in shape, were not at all uniform; there did not appear to be a standard size or any type of plan. Outside most of the premises there were advertising hoardings that were confusingly mixing with the road signs. Again most of these were colourful and all different in both shape and size. Ripped and faded posters adorned the lamp posts and power cables were strewn between the buildings in a most haphazard and untidy manner. But there was one thing that differed greatly from India…there was no accompanying mess. It seemed that despite their financial shortcomings the Peruvian people still had their dignity and sense of pride in their surroundings.

At 11:00 we stopped at a checkpoint for reasons unknown to me, but as we departed I noticed our speed was considerably reduced. For the next thirty minutes we must have entered a timed section of road where our average speed was monitored, because despite the clear and flat road ahead we were making very slow progress. Cars were now overtaking us with ease, which hadn't been the case earlier. This was particularly aggravating as we were also behind schedule.

We soon passed under the first of two large signs welcoming us to Cusco, but given the surroundings it was obvious we still had some way to go before we reached the main part of the city. The clouds had for the most part disappeared, leaving a sea of deep blue sky; the few that remained seemed to be almost in reach on the top of neighbouring hills. The sun was now nearing its peak, so without the cloud cover it looked like we were in for a very hot day.

We finally reached the Cruz del Sur terminal in Cusco at 13:00, an hour later than the advertised twenty-two hours. This meant that, for the one thousand kilometres we had travelled, our speed had averaged out at forty-three kilometres an hour. I had once spent twenty-three hours flying to New Zealand to attend a wedding. It was amazing to think this had taken the same amount of time, given the relatively short distance we had covered by comparison. At least on that occasion I had some decent inflight entertainment; the worst part of this trip had been the boredom. The coach had been comfortable enough, but understandably, I was now glad to get off and stretch my legs.

Luggage retrieval proved to be a most frustrating experience, as I had to wait longer than expected to be reunited with my bag. It had been one of the first to be unloaded, but then to my dismay, it was left to one side on the pavement. The porters' minds were focussed solely on the smaller bags, which they loaded onto a trolley before transporting to a holding area. All the bags (except mine, of course) were then placed onto racks behind a counter. The staff completed the process by reading out the names on the labels, so the owners could stake their claim. I had to wait until this part was almost finished before I could catch their attention and ask them to make another trip. The most annoying thing of all was that I could actually see my bag through the large glass window, while not being able to go and collect it.

My next challenge concerned the transport to my hotel. Internet research had led me to believe that there were no taxis at this dedicated Cruz del Sur terminal, which meant I would have to walk to the town's main bus terminus. Thankfully my luck changed at this point and this proved not to be the case. As I headed out of the exit I was immediately accosted by a local taxi driver. Despite the promise of more driving I was still glad to be on the move once more and I was most eager to see what Cusco had to offer.

Initially the long multi-lane roads were divided by grass verges in an attempt to bring some colour to the area. The surrounding buildings were fairly modern in design, although still not pleasing to the eye. When we were halfway to the hotel the area changed and became very industrial looking. At this stage I was starting to despair at the possibility of staying in such a horrible place. I had expected more.

As we neared the hotel we entered a one-way system, where the scenery thankfully changed for the better. The buildings were now three storeys high and all uniform; many were joined together, with only the doorways and small signs to distinguish where one ended and another began. The top parts of the walls were painted white, leaving exposed stonework on the lower half as a feature of sorts. The lower parts reminded me of country walls only on this occasion with cement joining the masonry together, almost a larger version of pebble-dashing.

I arrived outside the El Mercado hotel at 13:30, paid the driver S/.20 for the journey and entered the reception area. I noticed a small sign on the reception desk offering a massage service in the hotel for S/.130, but I decided to wait and see if there were local alternatives. They would undoubtedly be cheaper and by experience I have found that it is usually the same people. I completed the necessary paperwork seated in a room adjacent to the front desk, while sipping a complimentary soft drink (notably not Inca Kola), all very civilised and welcoming. Once these preliminaries were completed I left reception and went in search of my room.

From the outside, the building was very plain looking, but once beyond reception, I discovered a delightful courtyard complete with overlooking balconies. This space greatly reduced the capacity of the hotel, but I think on this occasion the designer had made a good decision. Guests would welcome somewhere to spend the warm summer evenings having a quiet drink. During the winter nights they could gather around the central fire, utilising the low benched seats provided. Even if it rained there were large umbrellas and a sheltered walkway allowing safe transit from the rooms to the reception. This looked just the place for me to relax and acclimatise after my daytime excursions; thankfully my earlier concerns had now proved to be unfounded.

My room was one level up from the ground floor so the porter used the lift to deliver my heavy suitcase. I, for my part, struggled on admirably with my laptop. Once inside I found my room to be a little snug due to a very large bed, but it had everything I needed. Opening a side door, I discovered I had access to an outdoor seating area, albeit shared by a neighbour; rather bizarrely though it was sited in an atrium void with no view at all.

With my essentials secured away in the room safe I didn't waste much time settling in. Despite my mild headache and nausea, I was keen to see what the centre of Cusco had to offer. After freshening up I left the hotel and headed for the Plaza de Armas (or 'Parade Ground', as in Lima). It was only a five-minute walk, which was one of the reasons why I had selected the hotel in the first place. Upon arrival I discovered a large paved square with three-storey-high buildings surrounding it. These buildings contained restaurants and shops, all with covered walkways on the ground floor elevation and similar to my hotel courtyard. The designer had included numerous random-shaped raised beds within the square, only one-brick high, which gave form to the pathways around them. These grass beds were bordered by yellow daisies and for additional height the occasional tree. The scene was completed by the benches sporadically scattered around the perimeter, allowing visitors to spend time relaxing in the space.

Although there were a lot of cars attempting to drive around the perimeter of the square, their progress was somewhat hampered by their numbers. As a result they crawled along, thankfully making little in the way of noise. It seemed to me that it would be better to pedestrianise the whole area. Although to be fair, from what I had seen so far, there was limited space to make that idea work. The surrounding roads were already busy and mostly one-way because there was simply no space for two cars to drive side by side. The planners of Cusco, just like their counterparts in London, did not foresee the invention of the motor vehicle or their great numbers, prior to designing their narrow-street city.

As there were multiple roads leading away from the square I took a stroll down each of them in turn, but only for a hundred metres or so. As well as looking at the shops I kept half an eye open for a nice restaurant. I was starting to feel a little hungry as I hadn't eaten much since yesterday morning. When I had my fill of walking I stopped off at the Inka Grill on the main square as the menu looked good and the place seemed quite popular.

I ordered ceviche to start, which was slightly different to the dish I helped make in Lima, mainly due to the additions of some salad items. Although it tasted good it was far too large for a starter, particularly as I also had a bowl of noodle soup to follow. Those two items would have sufficed if I had known, but I had also ordered a main course of trout and potatoes. I should have learned by now to order the courses separately in unfamiliar restaurants; I can then judge them for both their size and quality before deciding whether to continue ordering. Despite the size of the main course proving to be smaller than the starters I still couldn't manage it all. All the dishes tasted good, but the venue and the food presentation, had that tourist feel to it. With a bottle of water the bill came to S/.82; with my meal unfinished, I left S/.90 and departed.

I have often written about my dislike of tipping, but I will briefly touch upon it again. First of all, I have to say I do understand the concept. We are encouraged to recognise good service and reward the member of staff accordingly; it's the right thing to do. But then we are also told that some employees are poorly paid, so we should be helping these unfortunates by supplementing their wages, with no mention of the level of service; there is clearly a contradiction here. But my biggest gripe has to be with the practice of continuingly adding things on. While on my travels I have found that the Indians are the best at it. In Delhi I received a bill where I was not only charged for the food; they added VAT, then education tax, higher education tax and finally a supplementary tax on the type of alcohol I drank. Then they also wanted a tip! Overall it's too much to think about; I would prefer if the owners charged a little more and paid their staff better. Wouldn't that be simpler?

Before returning to the hotel I did find a place for a massage and it was indeed significantly cheaper than the hotel at S/.40. The room was very large, with curtained-off areas surrounding the beds. The privacy of the customers seemed a secondary consideration, particularly as the masseuses wanted to chat amongst themselves while performing their duties. Although it did feel good to relax for an hour, the skills of the masseuse were somewhat lacking. I think, rather than a place of relaxation, these sorts of places are just a source of employment for the locals.

Back at the hotel I made a big decision concerning my return trip to Lima. Although I did have a return coach ticket in my possession, it would have to go unused, as I couldn't face a repeat of that horrendous journey. As my laptop would remain behind in Cusco for the next week or so, I decided that now was the best time to make the alternative arrangements.

I booked a flight which would take about four hours, once I factored in the travel to the airport and waiting-around time. As a result of arriving early in Lima I would also need an additional night's accommodation in lieu of my coach 'bed'. Rather than add to my existing booking, I selected another hotel, as I didn't want to complicate matters; I also thought it would be good to see another part of Miraflores.

Once that was dealt with, the next thing to address was my luggage situation. Now was undoubtedly the best time to divide up my belongings as I had a really busy day planned for tomorrow; I had a full-day excursion and upon my return, the evening team meeting. I had read in the brochure that there was a weight restriction of 10kg, which was imposed to limit the amount the mules were allowed to carry over the mountains. It was good to learn that the welfare of the mules was being considered; it would have been easy for the organisers to have been more flexible just to please prospective clients.

When I carried my case over to the bed, I stubbed my toe on the wooden bed frame, keeping up my record of hurting my feet in every accommodation so far. I put my clumsiness down to the acclimatisation, as my head had been all over the place the last few days. After the swearing had abated I made a most unwelcome discovery within my case. It appeared that a bottle of sterilising fluid had leaked out onto some of my clothes. As well as the distinct chlorine smell, I noted that stains had appeared on some of my thermal tops. As the essential warm weather clothing was affected the most, I decided to entrust the hotel with some washing. I filled a laundry bag and put it to one side. As my time was rather limited I should have really taken it straight to reception, but I still had a mild headache and I wasn't thinking straight.

I then proceeded to reduce my belongings to the bare essentials, which proved more difficult than I first anticipated. I began with my riding gear, coat, casual evening wear, hat, camera, sunglasses, underwear and washing materials. I also had a plastic water bottle, which had been the reason I had brought the sterilising liquid in the first place. I thought at the time this sounded like aggravation, but all the same I dutifully followed the recommendation. The cleaning agent would remain behind, as I couldn't face another accident. Once I had everything divided up to my satisfaction, I moved the case off the bed and stacked the separated items on top. The fine-tuning would have to wait until I was in possession of the duffel bag.

I had intended to explore more of Cusco today, but the overnight journey and altitude sickness had taken a lot out of me. The lack of oxygen was affecting my mind, making me at times, a little befuddled; I was sure the lack of sleep wasn't helping either. In fact I think I did quite well to achieve the things I did today. I had been for a walk around Cusco, eaten, sorted my luggage and booked the much-needed alternative transport and accommodation. I should have tried to source some medication, but by the time I remembered I found sleep to be more important. I spent the rest of the day relaxing in my room, mainly catnapping. Tomorrow I was off to the Sacred Valley, following the much-trodden path of the Incas. Hopefully I would learn more about their way of life and have something positive to report.

CHAPTER FIVE

The Sacred Valley

I awoke at 05:30 to discover I was bright red in the face and had a slight headache – not the best of starts to a busy day. I didn't even have alcohol to blame for the condition; in fact, if I hadn't known what the problem was I would have been quite alarmed. At 3,400m I was now at the lower end of the altitude sickness scale, but the shortage of oxygen was clearly now having an adverse effect. As I drank a cup of coca tea I gave some thought to my day.

First on my agenda was my washing. I knew the hotel's S/.50 charge was significantly higher than the fee the locals would ask. I also knew where to find the nearest laundry services, as I had passed several during yesterday's mini-exploration. What I didn't have though was the time to deal with any problems, should they occur, as I was leaving early the next morning. The extra cost would on this occasion be for peace of mind, as the hotel staff would address any issues better than I, in the unlikely event they arose.

With that decision made, I headed down to breakfast, stopping by reception to inform them about the laundry bag left in my room. I could have brought it down with me, but I thought it better to leave it for the staff cleaning my room. It was early, and the night shift on reception would soon change shifts, so my things might get misplaced before the arrangements had been made. I did leave clear instructions that I needed it returning by 19:00 today, allowing just over twelve hours for the process.

I found the breakfast room in a basement off the main courtyard and despite there being no windows it was still welcoming; it had an arts and crafts feel to it as well. All the wooden chairs were painted green and fitted with white covered cushion pads. There was a row of tables along the back wall displaying the usual selection of cereal, breads and hot food. I sat at one of the small round tables and tried some more coca tea, even though I didn't feel the first cup had helped at all. I also took up the waiter's offer of a made-to-order omelette before visiting a manned stall at the entrance for a freshly prepared smoothie. This was probably my healthiest breakfast of the trip so far, which was not intentional – it just sort of happened.

At 07:30 I left the hotel and went in search of a local chemist. I knew I was cutting it fine, as I only had half an hour before I was to depart for my excursion. I hurried along to the shop recommended by the receptionist, only to inevitably find it had yet to open; fortunately it didn't take too long to find another. Despite my earlier concerns about the potential language issues I found the owner very receptive to my request and ever so helpful. Not only had he the solution to my ailment, he also offered to split a medium-sized box of tablets to reduce the cost. Now you don't get that in England! I declined his kind offer as I thought it would be good to carry spares; I could then leave some in my daypack and leave the rest in my pockets. At the same time, almost on a whim, I purchased a packet of coca leaves, all for a grand total of S/.5.

Back at the hotel I decided to take my small daypack rather than rely on the pockets in my sweatpants as they felt a bit too flimsy. I only took the bare essentials: money (but not wallet), suntan-lotion spray, bottles of water, sunglasses and camera. Most annoyingly though, I couldn't locate my hat (it was already in my daypack – too many pockets), but with no more time left to search for it I headed down to reception to await my tour guide.

Today's excursion focussed primarily on the Sacred Valley, which along with Machu Picchu and Cusco formed a major part of the Inca Empire. The valley was formed by the erosion from the Urubamba River, leaving fertile soil on its banks. As this is usually the case with rivers it makes me wonder why the majority of the Incas chose to live high up in the mountains and not exclusively in these types of fertile valleys.

My rep, Jose, arrived ten minutes late, a little out of breath and somewhat apologetic, but more importantly (and surprisingly) without a vehicle. After a brief discussion concerning Cusco's traffic problems I was invited to join him on a walk to the end of the street, where I found the vehicle waiting around the corner. As I discovered yesterday, traffic was a problem in these tight streets. It seemed worse in the mornings and early afternoons so it may have been partly due to the school run.

Once on-board the sixteen-seater minibus, I found myself among a small group of North Americans, mainly of East Asian descent. They kept to themselves to begin with, but that was to change as the day unfolded. They seemed familiar with the guide, judging by the way they spoke to him – a little 'over-familiar' at times. I was content to sit back and watch the world go by, listening to the guide when he had something interesting to say.

At 08:45 we arrived at our first stop: the Awana Kancha project, which takes a little explaining. The locals had set up a community scheme to showcase their skills in producing handmade textiles and clothing. When we first arrived I thought this was just going to be little more than a shopping trip, but I was soon pleasantly surprised to find so much more going on.

As I have previously stated I am not a fan of shopping trips at the best of times, so when they are factored in I am a little annoyed. In China, I had a small disagreement with a tour guide while on a trip to see the Terracotta Warriors. I had travelled overnight on a train from Beijing, arriving in Xian just after 08:00. I wasn't in the best of moods as I hadn't slept all night despite my having a bed in a private carriage. When I met the guide at the train station one of the first things he told me was that time was very limited and he seemed to be hurrying me along to the vehicle. Knowing there was a factory and shop visit planned I asked him to skip ahead to the main attraction. I had already viewed them on the internet and I wasn't really interested. My request was met with some consternation so I had to speak to his boss on the telephone. I explained to her that she was limiting my visit to see the real Terracotta Warriors, just so I could spend time looking at scaled-down replicas being sold in a shop. Did she not see the irony? I was unsuccessful with my plea as I was informed that a proportion of the guide's salary was paid for by the shop owner. So, although I didn't have to make a purchase at the shop, my attendance was a mandatory requirement or I would be charged more for the excursion. By the time I had finished the debate, in a most civil and calm manner it must be said, we were almost there. The driver had ignored my protestations, although I doubt he had understood them, and continued onward as planned. As I am sure you have already guessed this stop-off was very brief indeed.

Back at the Awana Kancha project, Jose began the tour with a visit to a stall containing hanging strands of dyed wool; there were dozens of different shades. The wool originated from the on-site alpaca/llama farm and the wide range of colours was developed from the many sources of natural dyes. For example, I learned they used lichen to make yellow or brown dyes depending on its age, indigo leaves to make dark blue dye and beetle blood the deepest red. I had never given the source of natural dyes much thought before, but I suppose it's a little obvious they originate from insects and plants.

Next we passed a local woman sitting at a hand loom, dressed in multi-coloured traditional Peruvian clothing. She was making a garment utilising the dyed wool from the adjacent racks. The item she was making would take weeks or maybe even months to finish rather than just a few minutes by machinery. Watching this labour-intensive process was fascinating; the repetitive nature of the task was mesmerising. However, the patience it took was incomprehensible to me as I crave variety in my life. Time was the reason given for the very high price of the finished product; I later found the on-site gift shop was testament to that.

There was the inevitable potato display (I never thought I would write that in a sentence) which comprised a few of the types in bowls. I quite rightly identified the oca, a thin yellow root-like potato, one of the types I had eagerly scrubbed during my cookery lesson in Lima. In appearance it looks like a large beetle grub with ribbed pale skin, only a lot tastier I suspect. At the back of the counter there were also glass cases displaying various coloured corn-on-the-cobs. I know now that these would be squeezed to make various drinks such as the purple chicha morada.

We were soon left to our own devices to wander around the project, arranging to meet back outside the gift shop in twenty-five minutes. I did take a quick stroll around the large two-room shop, without making any purchases. Photos weren't allowed to be taken of the inside which I found surprising, as this would surely be a form of advertising? Maybe they were worried someone might make cheap counterfeits of their designs from the pictures.

It didn't take too long for me to become bored with looking at clothes and so I headed off to visit the animal pens at the opposite end of the grounds. There were four types of wool-producing animal on display in their grass-floored corrals: Llama Ch'aku, Llama Q'ara, Alpaca Huacaya and Alpaca Suri.

Collectively they are the strangest creatures I have ever seen; it's almost as if they had been genetically designed to deliver a bespoke product. Some seemed to have far too much wool for their own needs; it was as if they were visually announcing that fact and inviting people to help themselves to the surplus.

After spending my remaining time viewing the source of the products the Americans were purchasing, I wandered slowly back to the meeting point. As the rest of the group exited the shop I directed them to the livestock, assuring them they had the time to take a look if they were quick – I would stay and await the guide. Jose should really have started with the animals before moving on to the dyed wool, manufacturing and sales departments. It would have a brought a 'soup to nuts' approach to proceedings.

Our next stop was at 10:00 for a photo opportunity overlooking the Sacred Valley itself. Looking down from our vantage point I saw the Urubamba River meandering through the valley; on either side there were flat grassy plains and mountainous slopes. I learned that the village of Coya, at the bottom, was created by the Spanish conquistadores. They understandably decided to move the people from the neighbouring hills in order to make them easier to manage. I can only imagine the indigenous population's sigh of relief at this development. There would be no more unnecessary climbing and the sparse dry mountain soil was replaced by a fertile alternative, fit to grow their crops.

As we stood and viewed the valley below Jose informed us that the Incas believed that 'precious' metals were symbols, with gold representing the tears of the sun, and silver, the tears of the moon. I wonder if this is where the elevated value of gold comes from – do we not value the sun more than the moon? The Spanish invaders had their own ideas, of course, as gold and silver meant wealth and power in their society. It was strange to learn that two sets of people revered the same items, but for completely different reasons. I wonder if the Incas had used other cheaper and less revered metals, to achieve the same goal, would they then have had fewer problems with the Spanish? These conquering expeditions had to be funded in some fashion – it wasn't the land or the people they were necessarily after.

Our next stop at 10:15 was at Pisac which had the most amazing market I had ever seen, but before we were let loose to explore there was of course a shop to visit. This wasn't a workshop or a factory; it was merely an establishment with wares to sell. As we were led inside I had that sinking feeling I get when I am asked to go shopping for unnecessary items. At the far end we were greeted by the shop assistant who, despite having a wide range of jewellery at her disposal, instead chose to show us a collection of coloured marbles.

They were shiny and round.

I stayed as long as it was polite, before heading out of the back of the shop to check out the empanada stall.

Unfortunately, just as I made up my mind to sample the wares, I discovered that I had left my money in my daypack. I had to leave the shop and go in search of the minibus, which took me a few minutes to find as the driver had moved from the drop-off point to a suitable parking space further along the road. Once solvent I returned and sampled two different types of the small, savoury pastries. They were tasty enough, but nothing special. I was more impressed with the enterprise of the vendor locating himself in the shop's back courtyard. If all the guides brought tourists into the shop, he must do a reasonable trade.

Once I had finished with my snacks I then took a stroll around the stalls. Despite my dislike of shopping this did seem the ideal opportunity for me to start (and complete) my purchase of souvenirs, presents and, just as importantly, a new hat. It was just starting to get warm and, in the absence of something to cover my head, I knew I was going to suffer at some stage today. Thankfully my headache and nausea had now subsided, thanks to the medication. Although at 2,972m I shouldn't have been having too many problems.

It was soon apparent that although there were hundreds of stalls in this square, there was actually little in the way of variety. Although this was a pleasing discovery, as I would have fewer decisions to make, it made me wonder how the vendors made their money. I tried to imagine myself sitting at the end of a row and spotting a potential customer. How optimistic would I be that the person would ignore all the other stalls and approach mine? The chances of my making a sale seemed slim at best. What I found most pleasing though was that the vendors left me to my browsing. These Peruvians were certainly no pushy salespersons, just simple folk sitting at their stalls watching the world go by. Some waved fans across their faces; others just sat staring vacantly into space. I have been to many countries where I would have been accosted as soon as I came into view and hounded until I left.

It took me longer than I had hoped to find a suitable hat as I had a particular style in mind. It had to be made of breathable polyester and have a wide rim all around the edge to keep the sun off both my face and neck. The majority I found on the stalls were made of a brushed felt material which made me feel hot just looking at them. They were also tall and pointed – if I was going for the wizard look, I was shopping in the right place. When I eventually found the type I was looking for I was a little dismayed to discover they all had Machu Picchu logos on the front, which looked a little tacky. All the same I needed a hat, so I chose one that was dark green on the outside and beige on the inside. The last part of my shopping spree went a lot smoother; I bought a couple of shoulder bags for S/.15 each, for my two nieces, Emily and Rebecca. I also purchased a ludo set, which used some typical Peruvian animals as pieces, for S/.20.

At 11:15, with our shopping complete, we were back in the minibus and on the move once more. As we drove Jose described the local, modern-day people in this area. Although the small houses in the area looked primitive from the outside, they all had piped water, electricity, telephones, and as we drove by I could see some even had satellite dishes. These are standard facilities in more affluent countries, but here it seemed at odds with what I had thought about the people of Peru. These villagers were supposed to be very poor and struggling to make ends meet. I now think that this is the perception they are happy to portray to outsiders, in return for tourist money, and who can blame them for that.

In the past the young people felt they had to leave these rural surroundings behind in order to find work in the big cities. Things have now changed for the better and they are now returning or choosing not to depart in the first place. I stated earlier as I entered the outskirts of Cusco that this region reminded me of India, but now I am not so sure; the tourist money seems to filter through to the Peruvian people a lot better.

At 12:15 we stopped at the grounds of a large hotel to have our lunch. To get to our outdoor seating area we had to first walk through their magnificent gardens, which were full of meandering paths, interspersed with colourful flower beds and well-kept lawns. The surrounding buildings were one or two storeys high with white-washed walls and half-round terracotta ridge-tiled roofs. Our lunch was served in an open-air, stand-alone group of structures; there were no sides, just thick wooden posts supporting the large gabled roofs. While sat at the tables the layout still provided us with excellent views of the gardens and allowed a rather pleasant cool breeze to pass through unhindered.

There was a quite a good selection of both hot and cold food on display, such as sandwiches, salads, pasta, bite-sized canapes, soup, rice, potatoes, stews, chicken pieces and many other dishes. The young Americans, fully conversant with buffets of course, attacked the tables with gusto. I, for my part, took a more conservative approach and returned with just the one, medium-sized plate of food. I was invited to join the rest of the group at their table and soon learned that this was a wedding/honeymoon trip. The Chinese-American man had just married an Argentinian woman and they decided to bring some friends and family along. His mother and father sat at their own table, occasionally frowning at the boisterous goings-on adjacent to them. Lunch lasted for forty-five minutes, which was barely enough time for my companions to complete their multiple visits to the tables.

Back on the road we headed for the ruins at Ollantaytambo which took around forty minutes to reach. This was undoubtedly the main attraction of the tour (if you discount the buffet) as these ruins were of historical importance to the Incas; I was beginning to wonder when we were going to see some of the ancient buildings. Jose informed us the original structure was constructed as a temple, but later, through necessity, it had become a fortress. Here the Incas won one of their very few battles against the Spanish, but it was only to prove a temporary reprieve. Incidentally, Ollantaytambo is also a popular destination as a train runs from here to Aguas Calientes, the town located at the base of the Machu Picchu Mountain.

Upon our arrival we stood at the bottom of the ruins looking up at the mountain with the sudden realisation that we had around two hundred steps to climb. I was so glad I had chosen to have a light lunch. The side of the mountain had been terraced by the Incas to help prevent erosion; they also did not want rocks to fall on the buildings below during earthquakes. These terraces were about two metres in height and two to three metres in depth and stretched about twenty to thirty metres wide, tapering in at the top. The steps for the pedestrians were a lot more manageable, weaving their way ever upward.

We stopped at the halfway point, to allow for photos and to have a well-earned rest. Jose then pointed to a neighbouring mountain, just off to our right, where some Inca grain stores were sited. They were clearly visible even from this distance, with their smooth-faced rocks standing out against the rugged mountain. The sloping pathways leading up to the stores also occasionally came into view. I had initially thought the Incas were hiding up in the mountains, hiding from rival factions who wished to prey on their possessions. But these grain stores were visible for miles and quite unnecessarily so. They must have located them up there for another reason; yes, it would have been dry, but surely ground-based, brick stores would have served the same purpose? Perhaps they wished for potential recruits to see the fruits of their labour; maybe it was a status symbol of sorts.

At the top we found the temple of the sun, made from a collection of very large stones, each weighing between forty and fifty metric tonnes. They had been transported from an adjacent mountain behind us, which must have been a huge undertaking. To get the gigantic stones down they first had to cut slopes, before conveying the stones down on wooden rollers made from whole trees. That had been the easy part. I could only imagine the difficulty hoisting them up the other side as I had enough trouble just walking up. Once at the top the stones had been hand-carved so the joints were practically seamless. This was achieved in part by rubbing the roughly hewn surfaces together; given their size it was some feat to create such a pendulum effect. Unfortunately the temple was never completed and large 'tired' stones, as they are known locally, lay about in random positions.

At 15:00 it was time to start making our way back down and as I slowly descended I took a look at the buildings in the valley below. There was a distinct mixture of very old and new, distinguishable primarily by their colour. The older original-looking buildings were grey and drab, the newer were coloured in pastel shades of yellow and red or simply painted white.

With the tour complete we awaited the minibus at the main gate; the driver had to park several streets away due to congestion around the entrance. The relatively early finish was to avoid the parade that was about to start; yesterday's tour had apparently got stuck for hours or so we were told. At 15:30 we reached the hotel where the Americans resided, and they quickly departed, possibly for afternoon tea. I was now alone with the guide and driver to continue the long journey back to Cusco. As I didn't arrive back until just before 17:00, I realised the group must have had a really early start this morning, due to a large detour to pick me up. No wonder they were so hungry – they probably only had time for one breakfast. Upon arrival at my hotel I gave Jose a tip of S/.50 and the driver S/.20.

Today's trip, although long and tiring, had been a fascinating experience, a really good introduction into the realm of the Incas. The highlight for me had been the Awana Kancha project. Even though it felt a little artificial in places, it was as close to experiencing real Inca life as I could get. The quality of the handmade items was truly exceptional and a credit to the individuals that made them.

The Ollantaytambo ruins were also memorable, but for different reasons. The effort in hauling the stones must have been an immense undertaking; it is a shame that it was never completed. I also learned that the life expectancy of an Inca citizen was forty-five to fifty years, which was hardly surprising, given most of that would have been hard labour. This revelation probably resonated with me more than the Americans, as at the time of the visit (and as I write) I fitted into that age category.

Once back in my room I was pleased to find my laundry waiting for me, but I still couldn't pack anything as I needed the duffel bag. As there were still a couple of hours to go before my 19:00 meeting I headed out for another massage. At 18:30 I was sat in the hotel courtyard, by the fire, nursing a couple of bottled beers. As I waited I glanced around at the groups of people and wondered which ones were to join me on my trek.

At 19:10 a rather flustered woman approached and ventured my name; to her obvious relief I positively acknowledged her query. I was then asked to accompany her to the basement breakfast room; it seemed I had been waiting in the wrong place for someone to make contact. The other groups sat around me were nothing to do with the trip after all. This was how, despite residing in the hotel and arriving early, I was late joining the briefing.

I was led to a table in the corner where I found my guide Leo, waiting patiently along with a guest, Melanie. I could tell she was a little annoyed that I had arrived with a beer; I think she assumed that despite my being late I still took the time to visit the bar, which hadn't been the case. After my apology I didn't elaborate, as I don't feel I have to explain myself to strangers. I was certain I was the most displeased of the three of us, as I hate being late.

Leo began by informing us that although the lodges had the full complement of people, only Melanie and I would be riding. This came as somewhat of a pleasant surprise, as at the time of booking I had been informed I would be riding alone. The others, who were attending another briefing across the room, were to hike the whole journey. I hadn't believed that to be an option when I originally looked into the booking, but I was still happy with the choice I made. Why walk when you can ride?

Leo went on to explain that we were to spend the first five days with the horses, with up to five hours per day in the saddle. Our chosen route, along the Salkantay trail, would be higher and more dangerous to traverse than the more popular Inca trail. There would be many narrow gravel tracks to navigate as we wound our way up, down and around. To one side there would be the safety of the mountain, on the other we faced downward slopes or sudden drops – something that did not bear thinking about. He made walking these routes sound dangerous and we were to tackle the journey sat atop unfamiliar horses. At this stage I thought it best not to think too much about it.

The end of day five would see the Salkantay trail merge with the Inca trail, where we were to leave the horses behind. Leo informed us that there were major concerns over the erosion caused by two-legged animals over the years. This wear and tear had led authorities to now limit the amount of people on the trails to five hundred per day. As it is also no longer possible to travel independently, this number must also include the guides and porters, further reducing the tourist quota. On day six, we would join the main group for the hike over the last of the mountains. Once this last trek was completed we would catch the train to our hotel in Aguas Calientes.

Leo further elaborated that, for those who miss out on obtaining a trail permit for the dates they require, it is still possible to visit Machu Picchu by train. The total number of people allowed on-site per day is two thousand five hundred, as agreed by the Peruvian government and UNESCO. Although this is an option, and a viable one for the less able-bodied, I think the journey across the mountains is part of the whole experience. So if you are capable of hiking or riding the trail, it is best to plan your visit well ahead to ensure your place is secured.

Day seven would see the whole group travel to Machu Picchu for a morning tour; those that hadn't booked the extra day would depart soon afterwards. As one of those that had booked the extension, I could remain and spend the afternoon independently exploring the site. I would then return the following morning to complete my visit, before the afternoon transit back to Cusco by train and minivan.

As our meeting drew to a close, Leo presented us each with a stainless-steel water bottle. He explained it would be essential that we kept drinking along the trail as the high altitude would dehydrate us. The air was so dry it would even take moisture from our intakes of breath; this dehydration was probably the reason I had woken red in the face this morning. There would be opportunities to refill the bottles in the lodges and a small amount would be carried by the guides on the trail. I wish I had known in advance we were going to have our drinking needs taken care of. I had only brought the plastic water bottle and some sterilising liquid because of the suggestion by the company; this now made my suitcase mishap seem even worse.

While Leo made enquiries about the loan of the duffel bags I was left to have a chat with Melanie. She was originally from England, but had moved to California many years ago and worked in sales. The conversation quickly turned to horse riding and it soon became apparent that one of us was very well practised and the other, well…wasn't. Given the level of danger before us I don't think she believed me when I told her about my lack of experience; I was struggling to believe it myself. As a parting piece of advice, she advised that as a novice I would be really in need of daily massages, to which I immediately offered my thanks.

"Not from me!" she exclaimed.

When Leo returned he was empty-handed as the main group had taken the last of the bags, but he did promise to drop ours off early the next morning. Before I turned in for the night I decided to have an evening meal. Melanie had departed straight away back to her hotel, presumably to brush up on her massaging skills, so I dined alone. As I departed the restaurant I did briefly meet Lewis and Jyl, two of the hikers in our group; we all agreed we had an interesting time ahead of us.

CHAPTER SIX

Hail, Caesar!

When I popped into reception I was pleasantly surprised to find a blue holdall waiting for me; Leo must have had a really early start this morning. All I had to do now was carefully load my belongings inside, which should have been a simple enough task given that they were already separated out. But as I began stuffing the bag I realised I had a problem, calculating the requirements in weight alone made no allowance for the size or shape of the items I was to transport. My riding hat, chaps and riding boots in particular were simply not going to fit. With time running out I loaded the remaining items into my daypack. I then gave the room one final check over before making the first of two trips to reception.

At the front desk I handed over my large case and, with no little regret, my laptop. I did give some thought to taking it with me on the trail, but it would have been shaken to pieces in a mule pack – not that I had room for it in any event. It usually goes with me so I can upload my photos on a daily basis and I do this for two reasons. Firstly, I like to view the pictures on a large screen at the earliest opportunity. There are some occasions when retakes are possible, if I am not altogether happy with the first attempt. Secondly, and most importantly, by transferring the pictures to the hard drive (and separate USB devices) I am improving the chances of the photos surviving until I get back home. With this precaution in place the maximum I would lose, due to a breakage or loss of my camera, would be one day's worth of pictures. On this occasion it would be about a week before I returned to Cusco and that made me a little nervous. To lose all those spontaneously captured moments was simply unthinkable. A future revisit to Machu Picchu was possible, maybe even on this trip, if I sacrificed other excursions. The trail, horse riding and lodges though were a different matter altogether; those photos would be lost forever.

Leo arrived twenty minutes later than our prearranged meeting time of 07:00, but for once I wasn't overly concerned by this development. We had a fairly relaxed schedule today – an hour here and there really made little difference. The late arrival was no doubt due to the traffic, but at least this driver had persevered and had parked directly outside. I clambered into the minivan to find Melanie already on board and nursing a leaking water bottle. The gifts from last night were made of stainless steel and looked well made, but it goes to show you never can tell. What was more of a surprise to me was the fact that I hadn't been given the leaking one.

Leo had only the two of us to look after this morning, as the others were heading directly to the first lodge with their own guides. I presumed they would be hiking part of the way, as the lodges were in a remote setting and they were on a trek after all. In some ways I wished I was hiking with them as it would have been an amazing experience. I had no regrets about my choice at this stage, just that unsettling feeling one has when entering into the unknown. Once my things were stowed away in the back we set off for the stables.

Along the way Leo did his best to point out items of interest, but as there weren't too many, the conversation very quickly turned to the horses. I learned they took between three and five years to train and were very carefully looked after by dedicated staff. The animals were also on a selection rota; once they returned from a trek they were given three to six weeks' rest. The horses selected today were carefully chosen for their fitness and suitability to each rider. Hopefully my horse was experienced and extremely forgiving, otherwise it was going to be an interesting time for both of us. I would also venture that he would need the full six weeks' rest when he returned!

At the time of booking I had been honest enough when I had revealed my lack of experience. I told them about my lessons, but I did keep everything as vague as possible. I was concerned at the time that if I revealed too much then they may not have allowed me to ride one of their horses. I know now that hiking would have been offered which, although not disastrous, as I would still be staying in the lodges, would still have been disappointing. Despite my justified apprehension I was still determined to ride the trail, as I do like to try new things. Besides, the time in the saddle was limited to just a few hours each day, so what could possibly go wrong?

At 08:45 we stopped off at an Inca archaeological site called Tarawasi, eighty kilometres west of Cusco. Leo informed us the structures were built as a resting place for Inca runners. There were several steps at the front leading up to the property; either side was a wall made of stones carved in multifaceted shapes. Maybe it was these shapes that were the key to the wall's strength, or maybe they had just found it easier to trim them so they fitted neatly together. The individual pieces did not require any mortar and left no gaps at all; even a sheet of paper wouldn't have fitted in the joins. This was similar to the stones from yesterday's Ollantaytambo ruins visit, only on a much smaller scale. Although this was just a wall, it must still have taken a considerable amount of time and effort to complete.

Once the stairs were traversed we crossed the grass to a large stone structure, which sported twenty-eight alcoves apportioned equally on two of the sides. They were high enough to stand in, with room to spare above my head. I was not sure of their purpose; they looked like doorways or large windows that had been filled in. I was beginning to wonder if this was indeed merely a resting place as they had gone to a lot of effort without actually providing facilities for the tired runners. I would speculate that it must have previously been built for something more important.

By way of contrast the surrounding accommodation buildings were somewhat derelict and looked as if they were built in a different era, many years later. Some had balconies which were on the verge of collapse and there were large gaps in the roofs from cave-ins. The outer walls were covered with a clay brown substance so I was unable to verify for certain if they were constructed by the original builders, but it looked extremely unlikely.

Last of all, we took a walk around the garden which was interesting for two reasons. First of all, Leo pointed out some cochineal bugs on the cactus leaves. As I learned on yesterday's trip, these tiny creatures are the source of red clothing dye used in the local clothing industry. I did wonder how they first discovered this particular insect would be the one to use until Leo squished one on a leaf. It was amazing to see how much blood it contained; it must have been a vampire in a previous life. The second interesting sight was a carving someone had made on a cactus; it was some kind of message (in Spanish) on the leaves.

Why would someone do that?

We left the site at 09:00, but only managed to drive another fifteen minutes before we were halted by roadworks one kilometre ahead of us. We spent an age watching a mechanical digger scrape the side of the mountain in an attempt to widen the road. With the car's engine switched off, and no air conditioning, it quickly started to heat up the inside of the vehicle. To make matters worse the roadworks were causing so much dust we were unable to wind the windows down. The only other option was to stand outside, but that didn't appeal to me as there wasn't any shade, there was the dust issue all around and I could see the traffic policewoman swatting mosquitos away.

After forty-five minutes, and much badgering of the official, we eventually got the all clear to proceed. This was due mainly to the queue of traffic behind us, and not a convenient moment for the workmen to stop. It seemed upon our arrival our solitary vehicle had not been of sufficient importance to call a temporary halt to the works. I wonder how long we would have waited if no other cars had joined the queue behind us?

After twenty minutes we stopped again, this time for our scheduled break. This short drive made the recent delay seem even worse, as we had been so close to our destination. After exiting the vehicle we were led though an empty cantina and into the premises' back courtyard. There we discovered we had been allotted a private space with our own refreshment table awaiting us. We had a large umbrella to keep the sun off our heads, so I took off my hat and attempted to cool down.

Shortly after helping ourselves to tea, biscuits and coca leaves, the owner appeared carrying some vegetable waste and gestured to us to follow him. He led us to an outbuilding, opposite the kitchen, and opened the door to reveal twenty or thirty cuy, scurrying around the floor. The owner threw them the long, scrap vegetable leaves and the creatures let out what sounded like squeals of delight before passionately tucking in. This was not too dissimilar to the Americans at yesterday's buffet.

Although mesmerising, overall I had mixed feelings about this exhibition. When it comes to food, I don't like to greet the thing I am going to eat, whether that is lobsters or crabs in a restaurant water tank, a cow in a field or guinea pigs in a shed for that matter. Cut it up, cook it and serve it at the table and I will give it a try, I just don't like to give the origin of the meat too much thought. I think a lot of people refuse to eat meat for this reason alone.

As we sat resting, our bags were transferred to another vehicle, which was to head towards the lodge. As I had a second bag I was soon summoned and asked to make some adjustments. I thought we must be near the stables so I changed into my riding boots, slipped on my chaps and carried my hat and hiking boots. The hiking boots I would fit in the saddlebags for today, the riding hat I would wear as soon as I was mounted. I then had the unenviable task of trying to squeeze the daypack into the already overstuffed holdall. Once I was fully compliant our luggage was then spirited away, while we set off in our vehicle towards the stables.

Back in England I had initially approached my horse-riding lessons with quiet optimism, but that soon changed once I was mounted in the saddle for the first time. It was only then that the enormity of my Andean challenge really began to sink in. I felt extremely vulnerable sitting atop that magnificent black beast, mainly due to the sense of being so far from the ground, and that was before we had even taken a step. Once in the training paddock my anxiety wasn't helped by the horse becoming restless. As my lesson had yet to begin I was at a loss with what to do when he decided to go walkabout. The young girl handlers looked on with either bemusement or complete indifference at my plight, momentarily leaving me to my own devices. Fortunately a fence soon barred the way; otherwise we would have wandered off into the distance, never to be seen again.

It was difficult at first to know how hard to pull back on the reins and how hard to kick the horse along. I didn't want to hurt the animal, well at least not at that stage. Later there were occasions when I cared less, particularly when he deliberately stood on my foot as I led him back to his stable. Over the weeks I gradually learned to make the horses stop with a squeeze of my knees, make them start and move a little faster by using my lower legs.

The reins shouldn't have really been needed for anything other than steering, but I occasionally needed them to help with stopping or slowing as my leg commands were being ignored. It didn't help that Guinness and the other horses selected for me were the largest, most stubborn creatures they had available. The majority of the group were children, a few of which were joined by their mothers. Their horses were all smaller, and seemed more disciplined, just my luck really.

Undoubtedly though, the most difficult aspect of all was the dismounting. Because of their size I had a brick wall to stand on to assist with mounting, but nothing in the vicinity to help me get off. Without assistance I would have had to jump off, which is actually a lot harder than it sounds; besides, the ground was uneven so the last thing I needed was to damage one of my ankles so soon before my departure. Eventually, with some help, I learned to keep my left foot in the stirrup, swing my right leg over and sort of slide off, releasing my left foot at the last moment. Not the most elegant of dismounts, but effective enough. Now in Peru, I would have to use my new-found skills over the course of several days; hopefully the lessons would prove to be of some use.

We arrived at the Coronilla Ranch at just after 11:00 and met Oscar, the most important member of our team. As well as being our head guide, he would also ensure the horses were fed, watered and rested, etc. He didn't speak English, but Leo was on hand to assist with translations so that wouldn't be an issue.

Melanie's horse was led out of the stable first and she confidently mounted before being led around the paddock by one of the stable hands. I think she was quite pleased to learn that her jet-black stallion was usually ridden by the owner of the stable. At home she owned a horse and went riding most weekends. I was beginning to get the impression that Machu Picchu was a 'nice to have' on her trip, rather than the main attraction. This was fair enough, because if I was a keen rider, I too may have been looking for interesting rides around the world.

It was soon my turn to meet my four-legged friend, and a chestnut brown stallion called Caesar was trotted out. He had been chosen for me due to his mild temperament and experience of the trail; I would soon find out how accurate an assessment had been made. The stable hand found a piece of high ground for me and manoeuvred Caesar into position so I could easily swing my leg over and mount him. Once in the saddle I immediately felt at ease, thanks in no small part to my lessons. It was a different feeling though, as I had transferred from large, stubborn 'cart horses' to this elegant and seemingly mild-mannered creature. Caesar was significantly smaller than my training horses and there was a reassuring calmness about him which quickly filtered through, helping me to relax. If the transition had been reversed I would have been in for a very difficult trip.

There was one drawback though to having trained on a less responsive horse…old habits die hard. We had only taken a few paces before I was admonished by Oscar (with Leo translating) for pulling back on the reins a little too hard, even though I thought my action had been a comparatively gentle one. Caesar had raised his head in protest at my action, emphasising that he was not used to such rough treatment around the mouth area. During my training in England I had occasionally needed all my strength to rein in the beasts, but this frisky bay only needed to feel the lightest of touches of the rein on his neck to move left, right or stop. It really was an amazing experience; at times I felt like laughing at how easy it was. When left to my own devices I initially zigzagged to the left and right as he was *too* receptive to my commands; it really was like having power steering.

Judging by Oscar's stares I quickly got the impression that if I fell off, he would come running to save the horse. Without question he was assessing me, sizing me up even before I mounted his horse. On this trip I would essentially be ballast, a parcel to be delivered from point A to point B. For his part, Caesar occasionally turned his head slightly to look at me, somewhat quizzically, but almost certainly with suspicion. With eyes on the side of his head, the movement was subtle but noticeable. It was bad enough with Oscar watching me, now I had a horse checking me out as well. Over the course of our time together I was able to judge my performance by how often Caesar found it necessary to repeat this action.

Once we were suitably accustomed to our horses, Oscar approached to make the saddle and stirrup adjustments. The saddle was adjusted first by tightening the strap underneath a little, now that it was properly settled in. The stirrups were more of a personal preference; if they were too high they would be uncomfortable and stress my knees; if they were too low I risked my feet slipping out. When all the adjustments were made and the handlers content that I had at least some degree of competency, it was time to depart for the first lodge. We set off in single file with Oscar's white Arabian leading, Leo's brown Arabian next, followed by Melanie, with me bringing up the rear. For the most part, this was to be the order we were to keep to for the rest of the trip. I think it would have made more sense for Leo to have stayed at the back to keep an eye on things. I took that as a compliment in a small way, but it probably wasn't meant as one...I have to get small accolades where and when I can, you know!

Travelling in last place had its advantages; it meant I could see how the other riders performed and they in turn would not spot any errors I made. I quickly noticed how spritely and elegant the other horses looked. The Arabians were a refined breed, upright and elegant and very light on their feet – the animal version of me I suppose. While Caesar was no slouch himself, he was definitely a lot more methodical in his approach. I sometimes found I had to gently kick him along into a quick trot to close the gap every kilometre or so. I had been pre-warned he liked to lazily drag his feet upon occasion and would need this encouragement. During my training back in England I had the opposite problem, as my horses would consistently get too close to the horse in front. I had to constantly slow them down or risk the horse in front kicking them in the head, which although deserved, would lead to my getting thrown off.

After two hours we stopped for a break, without question to rest the horses rather than the riders. It was getting rather warm now and I was not helping myself with my choice of clothing. As the weather was changeable I was advised to wear a waterproof jacket, but my decision to also wear a thermal top and jumper was backfiring a little. It would have been nice to 'go casual' like the guides – they wore bandanas around their necks and baseball caps on their heads (along with their clothes!). But, even if I were permitted to remove my riding helmet, which I doubted, I would be putting myself at risk. If I fell off I would be in need of the added protection to my head, so common sense was the order of the day; I was a novice after all.

Leo was carrying a backpack which contained a first aid kit, some spare water and more importantly our packed lunches. The individual packages held sandwiches, fruit juice, nuts, oranges and chocolate. The horses only had grass and water, so I think the humans had the better of that deal.

As we sat on a bench within a shaded and derelict-looking lean-to, I began to nurse my aching knees. They have been troublesome since I was a youngster due to playing far too much football. On this occasion the now familiar sign of ligament stress was being caused by having to constantly use my knees as shock absorbers at every lift and fall. This much-practised action was needed to avoid the forbidden bouncing action on Caesar's back. At other times my knees were being held in a semi-permanent, almost right-angled position by the stirrups, which was making me cramp up. I hoped we would continue to have these rest stops so I could continue to stretch out this issue. If the stirrups were lengthened and I did slip out, it would be difficult to refit them while on the move.

The pain I felt after dismounting for the first time reminded me of another trip I had made back in 2014. I like to set myself interesting challenges, so one day I decided to cross a country by bicycle. I thought I would attempt this challenge while I was still young and fit enough to try. After viewing a map of the world I chose Latvia for its comparatively small size and the fact I had never previously visited. I carefully planned a route, printed off Google Earth photos of key junctions and booked accommodation for overnight stops. I then corresponded with the owner of a bicycle shop who not only provided my transport and some local maps, but also offered plenty of advice.

It took five days to tackle the two hundred plus kilometres and it didn't take long to discover my knees were not really up to the daily punishment. After day one I decided to send my pannier of luggage ahead of me by taxi to the next hotel, as it was not only weighing me down, but also unbalancing me. As this proved successful I repeated the process for the rest of the trip. The daily target between hotels still took most of the day instead of the three to four hours I had originally planned, as I had to keep stopping to stretch my legs. I couldn't delay too long though as the taxi would be waiting at the hotels for payment. Then all I could do in the late afternoons and evenings was rest my weary bones, which was somewhat disappointing. But at least I did complete the challenge, which was my main aim.

After twenty minutes had passed it was time for me and Leo to depart, leaving the other two behind for a further ten minutes. The gap we would create would offer Melanie the opportunity to really put her horse through its paces in order to catch up. The mischievous part of me wanted to break Caesar into a canter as well, just to confuse Oscar regarding our distance ahead. But once again common sense prevailed; day one was not the time to take stupid risks. After only a few hours of trotting along winding, narrow paths, I had learned something important. Horses are prone to tripping in the same way people are. Although surefooted, Caesar had already stumbled forward a number of times over the extremely stony ground. Given the rate he could gallop at, the consequences of a fall would be significant for both of us.

Even if I managed stay on board, I had the prospect of Caesar falling on top of me, which was unimaginable. Oscar would no doubt be pleased if I broke his horse's fall, but…

At 15:45 the Salkantay Lodge (3,869m) came into view and I was glad of the assistance in dismounting. Once on the ground I could hardly stand, let alone walk, and I needed a few minutes to straighten myself up. By the time I had righted myself, the lodge staff had appeared with a refreshing cold drink and a damp towel for my hands and face. Melanie watched on silently as I gradually shook off the remnants of the journey. It was only then, she later told the rest of the group, that she believed my earlier confession of being a novice rider. I took that as another compliment, as it meant my riding skills couldn't have been that bad.

Overall, today's ride had been a fantastic experience; I had spent four hours in the saddle and I still had four more days to come! What attracted me most about the prospect of these daily rides was the sense of purpose they promised. I wasn't riding around in a circle as I had in my lessons back home. I was actually travelling from point A to point B and using a horse as my mode of transport. There was a real sense of achievement when I reached the final destination and thankfully I then had Oscar on hand to take back ownership of Caesar and attend to his every need. Reins and saddle were removed, water and food provided, before being given free licence to roam within the fenced premises. This arrangement was all I could have hoped for and more.

Before I could indulge myself with a hot shower I was required to complete the booking forms in the lounge area. This was to be a one-off exercise where I was required to provide my credit card details for important incidentals, such as beer, from the nearby bar area. My details would follow from lodge to lodge without having to book-in again and receipts would be provided upon each departure, all very organised. The food was provided as part of the package and prepared by the two dedicated chefs, who were to travel ahead of us each day and who we were yet to meet.

Once formalities were completed I withdrew to my room to find my blue holdall awaiting me inside. The zip had been cable-tied closed to prevent any interference and that initially proved a little troublesome to navigate. But once that was sorted I removed my riding gear, quickly showered and changed into some swimwear. The lodges had an outdoor hot tub, which would hopefully help to soothe my aching body.

Outside I found two American gentlemen already immersed in the large tub and we were soon joined by a young lady, all of whom were part of another group. There was enough room in the tub to seat twelve people around the perimeter. The Salkantay Lodge was the largest of the set and the only one that could accommodate more than one group. Once again I discovered people were hiking; in fact this group had no horse riders at all.

Melanie soon joined us, and it was then it dawned on me I was lucky she had chosen to ride this week. I had been told, months earlier, that a minimum of two persons was required for the ride before my booking could be confirmed. As the months progressed and the departure date neared, I had to make several commitments; the cancellations of which would have caused me a series of headaches.

After half an hour I left the hot tub and went for the first of my daily massages. I had made the booking as soon as I had arrived knowing we only had one masseuse travelling with us and a lot of people were staying in this lodge. Although I arrived at the correct time of 17:15, preparations were still being made. This made me a little anxious as I had a team briefing at 18:30 and after being late for the first meeting in Cusco, I didn't want to earn a reputation for tardiness.

After ten minutes I was invited in and the massage began. Overall I found it a little rough, but not in a Thai sort of way, with hard pressure being applied. It was the number of repetitions that was the issue; I counted fifty-four on one occasion and I had to tell the masseuse to stop and move on to another area. On a positive note she used hot towels (the preparation of which being the cause of the delay) in layers which did feel really good. After the hour was completed she spotted some sores at the top of my behind and applied some cream without asking. I don't think her English was good enough to have a discussion of that nature...but even so. The breeches I was wearing during the ride were a little loose and must have rubbed away some skin. I just knew that was going to be an issue over the coming days. My overall assessment of the massage is not going to be at all complimentary. The delay in starting was forgivable as the hot towels were most welcome. However, the number of repetitions in one place was completely baffling to say the least. I also entered the massage room with bad legs, but left with a bad back. Therefore, this was my first and last massage on the lodge to lodge part of the trip.

Leo's team briefing to the horse riders was to the point and informative. Tomorrow we were to have breakfast at 07:30 and leave an hour later. Packing would not be an issue as we were to spend another night, here in the Salkantay Lodge. This went against my previously declared wishes of riding with a destination in mind, but there was a very good reason. Tomorrow we were to spend some time at a higher elevation; this sampling of a new height was a proven method to help our bodies adapt to the altitude. There were also the added bonuses of spending time at a glacial lake, before attending a shaman blessing ceremony.

After the briefing it was time for dinner, so I wearily climbed the stairs to the dining room – it couldn't have been on the ground floor, could it? The other members of our group were already seated, but to both my and Melanie's dismay we were kept separate at our own small table with Leo. We asked Leo to address this, from tomorrow onwards, by ensuring we joined the others. It wasn't much of a chore for the staff to push the tables together. Although we had a separate guide, and were taking a slightly different route, we still considered ourselves part of a group.

The meal itself was a little disappointing overall, if I am being honest, and Melanie felt the same. The vegetable soup was OK, the chicken with mashed potato a little bland and a chocolate biscuit in lemon sauce to finish was a little too sweet for my tastes. I had expected more as the food was advertised as one of the trips highlights; hopefully it would improve as the trip progressed.

Not long after dinner, I began to feel extremely tired, so I retired to my room for the night without even visiting the bar. I spent the remaining time left in the day preparing for tomorrow's trip. I charged my camera, set out my clothes and, with no television to amuse me, went to bed. My room had a propane heater, which was switched off at night, and a hot-water bottle had been placed in my bed. Both these items indicated the room would soon get cold, not that I cared too much, I just needed to sleep.

CHAPTER SEVEN

The Glacial Lake

At first light I had a number of things to remember outside of last night's briefing before we set off. Firstly, I needed to take my tablets: an altitude sickness tablet for my head and stomach, glucosamine for my dodgy knees, and a general painkiller for minor back discomfort due to the massage. Thankfully this high-altitude part of the trip would only last a few days and my back would soon be better, otherwise I would start to rattle with all this medication. Next, I had to make a decision regarding my riding gloves. Yesterday I had taken them off during our break and not bothered to wear them again, but upon reflection I thought it best to persevere with them. The reins had knots to locate my hands and I just knew that would cause a problem over time. Lastly, I also decided to wear my padded cycling shorts under my breeches to ensure my sores didn't get any worse. I had real concerns I might have to call a premature end to my riding experience; I would have to monitor the situation and hope for the best.

Before we set off there was a commotion in the reception area. Upon arrival at the lodge it was customary for the hikers to leave their muddy boots at the door, ready for the staff to brush off the worst of the dirt. This morning, it seemed, one of the hikers (from the second group) had set off in the wrong boots! The missing boots' female owner was distraught at the thought of being left behind while the matter was resolved. After discussions were held, and she had been calmed sufficiently, one of the guides was dispatched by horse to track the offender down. It would have been easy to spot and approach the person wearing similar footwear, but they then had to be persuaded they were in fact wearing the wrong boots. I mean, if they were so similar that they didn't notice in the first place, how would they be distinguishable now? The horse riders had no such worries as our equipment remained largely dirt-free, given our elevated position and limited time on the ground. As a result we were allowed to keep our footwear in our rooms, out of reach of marauding hikers.

We left on time at 08:30, after the boot issue was resolved, and the last hiker had departed. As their expedition took longer to complete, they typically left up to an hour before us. Riding the trail meant we got to rise at a more reasonable hour and have the breakfast table to ourselves. We had an additional team member join us this morning, named Isaial, who was to accompany us on foot. His purpose at this stage was unclear to me, but he was to prove invaluable over the next few days as we traversed the narrow mountainous sections.

Soon after leaving the lodge we undertook our first major uphill climb which meant I had to adjust my seating position. I was advised by Melanie to lean forward as far as I could. This helped with balance even though it felt a little uncomfortable on my stomach. I could now feel every jerky step Caesar took as we plodded along.

After an hour of this steep uphill riding we stopped at the bank of a stream where Oscar dismounted to clear some small rocks away. It appeared he was taking the precaution to protect the horses' lower calves from scrapes, something I hadn't previously considered. Most of the horses decided to take on water here; the riders had little choice in the matter once their minds were set. Not that we would have intervened of course, as this trek was hot work for the beasts.

Once across the stream we entered a plateau where we encountered a field of cows. As we rested the horses the cows slowly ambled towards us, mistakenly thinking we were bringing their weekly salt ration. Cows need salt in their diet or they soon lose their appetite and decrease in weight, no doubt upsetting the farmer.

While on the subject I am now going to have a brief rant about the use of salt. Humans, like all animals, need their ration, but in general terms our packet and tinned foods are loaded with excessive amounts. I then see people adding it to their food while cooking before inexplicably adding more once it is on the table. This practice is extremely bad for the heart. I watch chefs on television try to tell me (us) that this 'seasoning' brings out the flavour of the food, but they are talking utter rubbish. You add salt in the quantities they do and the food tastes of salt, nothing more. I personally enjoy the natural taste of the food; my joints may be failing, but I still have a refined palate.

Leaving Melanie alone to find a 'happy rock' (in lieu of proper toilet facilities) I took a stroll around the area. Today, for the most part, we were travelling across wide open plains, which presented me with the opportunity to take a good look at our surroundings. Apart from the cows I saw no other life at all; this really was a desolate looking place. The grass seemed to do nothing more than slightly colour the rock, it was so sparse. I could see snow on top of the highest mountains, some of which must have recently melted as I could see some of the rocks beneath were completely devoid of grass. It would have been easy to get lost without our guides as there were no obvious trails to follow. The dried-up river bed that meandered its way through this valley acted as a reference of sorts, but only if you were familiar with the route in the first place.

At our next stop we had to leave the horses behind with Isaial and Oscar as the trail ahead was too steep for them to ascend. Leo led us on foot up a very steep hill, which took us forty-five minutes to climb. Despite our leisurely pace we arrived at the top a little breathless and looked down from the summit upon the Humantay Glacial Lake. We were now at 4,300 metres, which was apparently a really good acclimatising height. I was feeling a little nauseous and as usual this was combined with a mild headache. The tablets I was taking only seemed to be taking the edge off this malady, maybe there was something to be said for the coca leaves after all.

Several months earlier I had been scanning through the brochure and read there was an option to go for a swim in the lake. I was definitely not going to pass up that opportunity, so after finding a large rock, checking first that it was not of the 'happy' variety, I quickly changed into my swimming shorts. As I tentatively entered the water I discovered it was indeed ice-cold. Well it would be, wouldn't it, being a glacial lake in the shadow of a snow-capped mountain! I sensibly had also remembered to bring sandals to prevent my feet from being torn to shreds by the sharp stones. What I hadn't allowed for though was the slipperiness of these stones; once or twice I nearly fell over when the water was only at ankle height. The last thing I needed now was cut legs to go with my other problems.

Deeper and deeper I ventured, from knee depth to waist height, until I was finally up to my chest in the ice-cold water. At this point the cold temperature took my breath away and I had to gasp just to regain my breath. Cold water is often refreshing to bathe in, but not in this case. After a few minutes I made my way back to the shore and the relative warmth of the rocks. Melanie remained on dry land taking photos of me with my camera, making comments like, "Only mad dogs and Englishmen..."

With playtime at an end I dried off and changed back into my riding clothes just in time to see the hikers from our group appear over the rise. Some did venture into the freezing cold lake, but somewhat reservedly only up to their ankles. Later at dinner they declared that it was not that cold and awaited my reaction...I demonstrably begged to differ!

The timing for us all to be assembled together at the lake was of course not a coincidence; we were there to take part in a shamanistic ceremony. Leo must have decided someone in our team needed a good luck blessing…I didn't think I was riding that badly!

Before the guest of honour arrived, we received a pep talk from Leo. I could tell from his demeanour that he was a little concerned that we would not take the ritual seriously enough or, worse still, bring a degree of ridicule to proceedings. As he spoke he pensively glanced around trying to read the expressions on people's faces. He needn't have worried as we were all mature individuals. I assumed that offending the shaman would reflect very badly on him so I understood his concern. While I am not remotely interested in these types of ceremonies from a spiritual sense, I am tolerant and mindful of others who are. Besides, as good as the riding was, it was nice to have a break and I was in no rush to return to the lodge.

Initially I thought shamans were like the witch doctors in Africa, but I have since learned they operate on the spiritual side, rather than dancing around shaking a stick at the world and working with potions. They supposedly have contact with good and bad spirits, influencing their impact on the living world. I am not sure if their communication methods have changed over the years, but these Peruvian shamans now have their own website. Presumably this is how the living keeps up to date with their services.

The 'Payment to Mother Earth' ceremony began with the shaman providing us all with multi-coloured hats, which were unmistakeably of Peruvian origin. They fitted snugly with long flaps to cover the ears and at the bottom of the flaps there were long tassels attached. The decoration was completed by a string of fluffy coloured balls connected at the very top. No doubt they were all made by hand which would have taken a lot of time and patience to complete.

When we were all correctly dressed the shaman then gave each of us an individual blessing, speaking in the ancient language of Quechua. I could only make out the words 'Machu Picchu', but we learned from Leo that he was wishing us a safe journey to our ultimate destination. Time would tell if his blessing had in fact protected us from the evils of the world.

Once the blessings were complete the shaman spread some paper down upon his blanket and proceeded to add all manner of bric-a-brac. The items were all no doubt symbolic, but I was a little surprised by the types he used. There were shop-bought biscuits in their packets, plastic coloured beads, a plastic toy (?) as well as the more predictable items like salt (more salt) and grasses. I had expected them all to be traditional items used in the past by the Incas. Once completed, the items were all wrapped up into a neat paper parcel, before being covered in the shamans' blanket.

I don't believe in this type of thing because I like to think I have a rational mind, but I do hope this ceremony continues as I do like traditions. As a link to the past it shouldn't be lost and be replaced with a latter-day equivalent. I just wish they hadn't sold out and started using plastic items and shop-bought biscuits; I wouldn't put them forward as good examples of what 'Mother Earth' had to offer. If there was a minute piece of credibility in the process it was lost to me at that moment. The final part of the ceremony would be carried out later this evening, back at the lodge, when he visited to sell us the hats we were wearing.

Did you see that coming?

As we sat down to lunch at the lodge Leo asked me if I was feeling OK, but as I wasn't, I asked to speak to him alone after we had eaten. The sores on my tailbone had gotten a lot worse and despite visiting the masseuse for more cream (no massage!), I really needed first aid. So, rather embarrassingly and with little choice, I had to retire to my room and show Leo the issue. He was fine with it though, having no doubt encountered this problem a number of times. With some more cream, wadding and tape applied, I was as good as new – well, as good as could be expected. Unfortunately, this now prohibited me from joining the others in the large outdoor hot tubs for the rest of the trip as I had to keep the dressing dry. I even had to be careful to wash around it each day in the shower. The alternative was to have Leo visit my room every day to reapply, and that wasn't going to happen, even if he offered.

After lunch I packed my bag ready for tomorrow's departure and headed to the bar for a well-earned glass of beer; ceremonies and stressful treatments make me extremely thirsty! I did enjoy the bottle of Cusquena I sampled in Lima, and it was on offer here, but on this occasion I chose to have a bottle of Erdinger Dunkel (dark), a German Weiss beer, instead. I had first tried this beer in Beijing, where the Chinese brewed it under licence, and it is very good.

Not too much riding today then, but I had survived another journey. Although there were no narrow passes to traverse today (they was still to come), I still found the ground full of stones and difficult in places to navigate through. Caesar had proved to be a good companion so far, an excellent choice by the handlers. As I was fairly new to this type of expedition I needed all the help I could get.

There were lessons for me to learn along the trail, lessons that no one thought to advise me of. For example, I had to quickly learn that it was my responsibility to check the trail ten metres or so ahead and select the best overall route. Caesar would, for his part, focus on his front hooves and pick his way through the stones to avoid stumbling and scraping his legs. We were a real partnership, working in tandem. I was now of the opinion that horse riding is not as difficult as I had initially feared, despite my aches and sores. We were riding at a nice steady pace, so there was time to look around and enjoy the surroundings. I even occasionally managed to take some videos as we rode along; I just had to keep one eye out for Oscar. But despite my early success I was not going to get too complacent as there was still a long way to go and things can change very quickly on the trail.

That evening the shaman arrived as promised and spread his wares out on the floor. He did have quite an impressive range of items available: hats, shawls, blankets and bags were all on display. All were handmade by the locals, brightly coloured and, unsurprisingly, very expensive. I bought a hat for a princely sum of S/.200. He didn't bat an eyelid when I repeated the price to make sure I had heard him correctly. I wasn't sure if the shaman was working on behalf of the locals by offering to sell their merchandise for them or whether this was a solo endeavour. I guess I would never know.

After our dinner and briefing were complete, Melanie and I were instructed in the art of Pisco sour making. Once the barman revealed the recipe (Pisco, lime juice, sugar syrup, egg white, ice cubes and angostura bitters) we were asked to decide on whether to stir it in a blender or simply give it a good shake by hand, a bit of a James Bond moment. The shaken version is obviously a little stronger as it does not infuse the watery ice as much. I was still in two minds about this drink. I hadn't particularly taken to my free sample upon my arrival in the country or to this one here. Pisco as a brandy is not a bad drink, but I do prefer it with the ginger ale. However, I didn't let on and dutifully consumed the one I made through somewhat gritted teeth.

Incidentally, given that this drink is so popular in Peru, I wonder what they do with all the remaining egg yolks. They must make a lot of custard because it wouldn't be in their nature to simply throw them away.

It was soon dark enough for the last part of our ceremony to begin, so the group was rounded up and directed outside to a nearby fire pit. Some of us wore our new hats; the others, who hadn't made a purchase, were not presented with temporary samples I noticed. Hopefully they would still have a safe journey. We all respectfully shuffled around the confines of the raging fire pit and presented ourselves in front of the shaman for one final blessing. When all the individuals had been blessed the paper parcel was removed from the blanket and tossed into the fire. With the ceremony completed, the shaman withdrew, walking a bit lopsided with one pocket full of our money.

Leo, who knows a fair bit about the stars and astrology it seemed, pointed out the Southern Cross and other constellations in the night sky. He used a laser pen, which worked surprisingly well; hopefully there were no aeroplanes passing overhead at the time. On the trail he had also pointed out various types of orchids to Melanie, as she showed some interest. The modern-day Peruvians seem to be really in touch with nature and their surroundings in general. I think this is true of all people who have little in terms of material wealth; they seem humble, more grateful and content with life. Not a bad way to live I suppose.

With the evening's entertainment at an end we each retired to our rooms and turned in for the night. Tomorrow we were heading to the smaller Wayra Lodge and another step closer to Machu Picchu.

CHAPTER EIGHT

Journey to Wayra Lodge

I visited the toilet at 02:30 this morning and did not go back to sleep after that as I find it difficult to sleep in strange places. We were advised to bring a torch for our night-time toilet breaks as the electricity would be switched off at around 22:00. Without knowing the layout of the lodges, prior to travelling, I had visions of night-time forays to an outdoor wooden shed. Thankfully the rooms all had their own private bathrooms closer to hand.

The power to the lodges was supplied by generators, run by fuel transported by the pack mules. The cost of the fuel was no doubt the major factor behind the decision to switch the appliances off at night. So, with this in mind, I was a little surprised to find the lights still worked at this hour. Which was an unexpected bonus as I realised I would have needed a light to find my head torch. Later I was informed that one of the other guests had need of overnight power for medical reasons, presumably there was an appliance to be kept on charge.

At last night's briefing we were informed that Isaial would again be tasked with scouting ahead today. He would be peeking around blind corners, looking out for the mule trains. As the paths were narrow, it was essential that when the mules approached at speed, we stopped and waited on the mountain side of the trail. Failure to do so could result in us being pushed off the very steep-sided mountain into the shrubbery far, far below. We really needed his advance warnings to carry out our manoeuvres, as the horses would not sense the danger until it was too late. To emphasise this point we were told that pack mules were killed, through falls from these very passes, on a regular basis. I hadn't considered this particular danger until then. I thought I had enough to worry about just handling the horse, without having to look out for mobile hazards.

At 07:30 I dropped off my blue holdall at reception and went along to breakfast. My belongings, along with several others, would later be transported by mule to the next lodge. The mules were scheduled to arrive at each lodge before we did, assuming they survived the journey. In terms of organisation I was quite impressed with all the arrangements so far. The lodges opened in 2007, to serve the sixty-three-kilometre trek, so the path was a well-worn one by now. They had nearly ten years to bed in and iron out the problems before my arrival.

As we were leaving the lodge we found the barman and maids standing outside the main door awaiting our thanks and goodbyes. The Mountain Lodges of Peru were required to employ members of the local community, in return for the permission to build and run the lodges. The staff members were rotated on a regular basis to allow as many people in the community to participate as possible. It was nice to learn about this type of arrangement because businesses of this nature shouldn't be all about money for the few. I should have asked about the rotation policy – I wonder how often a local could expect to work in the lodges. Would an intermittent arrangement interfere with other jobs? But maybe there weren't that many jobs to go round in the first place in these barren areas. Tips to the lodge staff were included automatically as part of my package.

Isaial had really drawn the short straw when it came to being allocated a job. Not only was he to keep up with the riders on foot, which was no mean feat, but he also had a dangerous task to perform. I can imagine the locals all lined up and a selection process being undertaken:

Official: *"You…barman."*

Official: *"You…maid."*

Official: *"You…go look for mules on mountain, bonus if you survive the month."*

We made several stops in the first hour to allow for individual photos to be taken – the mountain backdrops made for some stunning pictures to add to my swelling collection; although some of the locations were a little precarious. I think Caesar had trouble understanding why I wanted him to deviate from the safety of the path to go and stand right near the mountain edge. I then of course had to further persuade him to stand still while the photo was being taken, which was a real test of his good temperament and my handling skills.

The trail today was similar to the one we traversed yesterday; there were dirt paths littered with small stones and for the most part a slight incline. Occasionally we encountered flat plains containing enormous boulders which had, years before, fallen from the mountain tops. These were particularly difficult to navigate around and took a lot of concentration as I had to plan our route well in advance. On several occasions I came to a dead end and had to backtrack a little, but at least here there was little in the way of danger.

I was now in the habit of drinking from my stainless-steel water bottle without having to be reminded by Leo. Without his earlier prompting I would have forgotten about the dehydration factor altogether. I just had to be careful to time my moments as this task required the use of both of my hands to hold the container while unscrewing the lid.

It would have been nice to know exactly when we were going to stop for our breaks, from a pacing perspective. We seemed to be stopping at pre-planned locations, instead of assessing the needs of the riders and horses on an individual basis. While hiking it would have been easy to check on how people were feeling, but on horseback it was more difficult. It would not be at all apparent to Oscar and Leo that I was either cramping up or a little saddle-sore. We were together, but separated, by our single-file formation and distance from each other.

I did occasionally take my feet out of the stirrups so I could fully extend my legs for a few moments. I just had to ensure we were travelling slowly enough so I didn't have to apply the 'rise and fall' technique where I would need the purchase. At times I felt I had an ever-moving goalpost ahead of me and then, when I had almost abandoned all hope, we would unexpectedly stop. Don't get me wrong, I was still enjoying the ride, not simply enduring it; it just would have been nice to know about the stops in advance so I could pace myself better.

I was gaining more confidence with the reins, now only holding them in one hand, in fact just using my right-hand index and middle fingers to steer and stop. I even managed to hold my camera in the same hand, with the camera strap fitted tightly about my wrist. My left arm I let dangle by my side, in the most relaxed position I could be in. But in truth there were times when I still felt a loss of control was only moments away. I noticed that Leo's and Oscar's reins were much longer than mine. This meant they could use their left hand to steer and use the additional length in their right hand to whip their horses' hindquarters to speed things up. It was probably just as well I didn't have this option.

At Suyroqocha, our second rest stop, there was a sign informing us we were now at a lofty 4,480m. I still had mild altitude sickness symptoms at this stage, but nothing to complain about really. As we rested we were informed that the Salkantay Pass was less than one kilometre away and that was as high as we were going to rise on this trip. After that we still had mountains to tackle, but at least they would be at a lower altitude and I could stop taking the tablets.

When we reached the top of the Salkantay Pass (4,630m) I found the view spectacular. The clouds were really low and it seemed like we were riding through them; the misty atmosphere had an eerie, almost magical quality to it. Unfortunately, this also meant it was difficult to take decent photos, as the surrounding clouds were obscuring the very tops of the mountains.

Not long after we arrived the hikers appeared over the horizon, the timing intentional once more as we were to have lunch together in a large tent, a short distance away. The remaining journey to Wayra Lodge was presumably too far for them to walk, but I think the riders could have made it easily enough. The hikers were obviously travelling a different route, because we would have caught up and overtaken them despite their one-hour head start. Maybe we were riding a more circular route to avoid covering the distance between lodges too quickly.

Before setting off to the tents we had to wait for a heavily laden mule train to pass through. They were transporting propane containers for heating and what looked like large sacks of grain. They were accompanied by their handlers who remained at the rear of the train, doing nothing to actually steer them. No warning was given as they approached, but it was obvious we were to stay well clear. It was amazing to see them up close, trotting along the trail seemingly oblivious to the weights on their backs. Hopefully they had a long rest at the end of the journey, but I would never know for certain.

I am sure that Isaial empathised more than most, being the human equivalent amongst our team, although he had no load to carry on his back to slow him down. With some thought I am sure I could have found something for him to carry, maybe something useful for our rest breaks like hammocks or bottles of beer or even extra water so we could bathe our feet.

As we approached the campsite I spotted several tents, all with orange roofs and blue side panels. There was one large communal tent set aside for dining, another for the chef's kitchen and lastly a couple for toilets at the back of the site. I didn't check out the toilet facilities any further so we will just have to use our imaginations regarding their cleanliness. I found the lunch tent a little claustrophobic at first, until I was seated and the roof moved further away. The light passing through the orange canopy gave the interior a strange kind of glow.

We began the meal with soup, to which I added a spicy salsa mixture, just to give it a kick and make it a bit more interesting. This was soon followed by linguine pasta and there were poached pears to finish. All in all, this was a well-balanced, tasty meal and certainly an improvement from the first day. This was a little surprising as the chefs presumably had only the most basic of facilities here, out in the wild.

Coca leaves and coca tea were available on the table for medicinal purposes. The guides advised that while it was legal to consume them while in Peru, it was illegal to take them out of the country. As a group we discussed the claims that they counter altitude sickness, but I still wasn't convinced. Without the tablets I would have been suffering even with the coca products, of that I was sure. Another slight on Peru, I know, but not intentional!

The riders only took another hour to descend into the valley where Wayra Lodge (3,920m) awaited. Just as I dismounted it started to rain; it was as if the gods were watching over me. The shaman had now earned his money as far as I was concerned. I did spare a thought for the hikers…but there is only so much laughing you can do without attracting attention.

Wayra Lodge was about half the size of the Salkantay version, although similar in design. I was glad the owners hadn't agreed to the use of a standard template when constructing the lodges. Here there were just the six bedrooms (all with private bathrooms), a communal seating area with bar, kitchen, a separate dining area and an outdoor hot tub. All we really needed.

I briefly checked my room to make sure my luggage had arrived and kept up my 100% record of stubbing my toe in every bedroom I had stayed in on this trip. My bed at home doesn't have legs; if it did I would have cut them off by now. Returning to the bar, I once again sampled the Erdinger, only this time I had to settle for the blonde version as that was all they had; it was OK, but not as good as the dark.

I have to report that my padded cycling shorts were working extremely well; I only wish I had worn them on day one. They did look a bit ridiculous as the padding swelled out the back of my breeches, but I am sure this fashion indiscretion largely went unnoticed. The hikers departed the lodge before I even had breakfast and did not arrive back until after I had changed, so my audience was therefore somewhat limited to my small team. I continued to adjust my dressings whenever I showered, which was a pain from a functional perspective. The sticky plaster was getting harder to re-affix as it was starting to lose its bond. I really would have been better off having new dressings applied every day, but modesty would not allow any further third-party assistance. Leo had indeed offered to help, but I declined his kind offer and managed by myself.

For lunch and dinner we were now seated as a group and would remain so for the rest of the trip. It was nice to sit and chat with new people, listening to their take on the adventure. The whole group were couples, except for Melanie and me, and all were originally from the USA. I did ask them why so few of their countrymen travel abroad – it is said three quarters of Americans don't even have a passport. The answer I received was a plausible one. They were typically only given two weeks' leave from work (excluding Christmas) and most spent the time visiting relations who are scattered all across the country. The distance covered, in some cases, was similar to a European jaunt across numerous borders.

So the new members of the team, for mealtimes at least, comprised Jyl and Lewis, Amy and Erwin, Alberto and Marcy, and Frank and Olga. Their guides Whilder and Claudio also joined us and were very much the youngsters in the group, at half our age. There was much laughter at the table and not just when the alcohol flowed. I was fortunate to be travelling with such good-natured company. One of my concerns prior to booking was that the rest of the group might all know each other, and I might then have been the odd one out. But, even if this group had all known each other, I don't think they would have treated me any differently. There was a politeness that appeared to come naturally. While I don't think everyone was the best of friends, there were certainly no arguments or ill feeling; it could have been a lot worse. Leo joined us for dinner of course, but Oscar and Isaial ate in the separate staff quarters, where all the guides slept in bunkbeds.

It was now noticeably cooler at this altitude and I was struggling to get warm. Once the adrenaline had worn off from the ride and my coat was removed, I cooled off rather quickly. Drinking cool water and cold beer wasn't helping either so I tried a cup of tea and sat near the log fire which helped a little.

At 18:00 it was time for the riders' meeting to discuss tomorrow's schedule. There seems so much to remember on this type of trip, a bit different from staying in a hotel where I just had to worry about which clothes to wear and the contents of my pre-planned agenda. I found I had to constantly think ahead or remember something I was told at these briefings. Once again I had to pack and drop my bag off at reception, sort out my dressing and the time for breakfast. At least my back was no longer hurting so that was one less tablet to take.

Tomorrow we were headed for the Colpa Lodge, which sits at a lowly 2,800m. This of course meant that after tomorrow morning I wouldn't need the altitude sickness tablets until I returned to Cusco. It was still hard to tell how effective the tablets had been; to truly know, I suppose I would have to complete the journey once with them and again without. However, given that altitude sickness is a genuine condition and the fact that I was only experiencing mild symptoms, I would have to conclude that they were indeed helping. Still, it was good to know I wouldn't be taking them for much longer.

The riding time tomorrow would be approximately four hours, which in some ways felt a little short, being the experienced horseman that I now was. Leo advised that we were also going to ride along several narrow trails, which would test my new-found abilities to the fullest. Up until now the paths had been fairly wide and manageable, so tomorrow I would have to keep my wits about me.

Dinner was once again a very civilised affair; the long table had a heavy white linen tablecloth, sparkling glasses, white linen napkins and stainless-steel cutlery. Tonight's three courses included soup, beef medallions with rice and a fruit crumble for dessert. I bought another bottle of Erdinger, only to nurse it for two hours; the high altitude was affecting my appetite for alcohol in a most negative way. Most of the others drank wine, with red proving to be the most popular.

Although most of the others appeared to be seasoned hikers, they too must have been getting tired by now. Walking these long distances is one thing, but these uneven trails makes for difficult going and different muscle groups would be used. I had that all to come on my hike, but thankfully only for the one day. We all went to our beds at 21:00; after my very early rise this morning, I welcomed the rest.

CHAPTER NINE

Journey to Colpa Lodge

My list of ailments seems to be changing by the day and I now have a bruised tailbone to add to the ever-growing list. This must have happened on the rare occasion when I lost my tempo and bounced a few times in the saddle. It seems I would have to keep taking the painkillers after all. There is definitely an art to riding well; it is all about timing the rise and fall on a consistent basis. Caesar has his own rhythm worked out, so I just need to get in sync with him. If I am getting injured, his back must be feeling it too, hence his need for a lengthy rest at the end of each trek. My sore doesn't seem to be healing, but at least the wound appears to be clean and not getting any worse.

On a positive note, I know now I will be able to complete the horse trek; I am over the halfway stage and although I may be sounding a little negative at times, it really isn't that bad. In fact, once in the saddle, it is most enjoyable as each day feels like an adventure. My horsemanship is coming along nicely and, despite my understandable minor bangs and scrapes, I feel I am coping extremely well. I have occasionally broken into a fast trot, particularly when catching up with the others. I can feel Caesar wanting to step up another gear or two, but thankfully he is still responding to my wishes to ease back down, at least for the time being.

When I joined Melanie and Leo for breakfast at 07:30 I was a little tired, having awoken once again several hours earlier than was required. The hikers continue to depart on their earlier schedule, so I still see nothing of them in the mornings. For a change I tried an American breakfast of pancakes, with blueberries and some fruit. Our buffet is very basic, but the chefs will cook a variety of one-off requested items as well. The food has certainly improved from the first day, but not to the extent of the post-trip reviews I have read; it is varied and good, but not exceptional.

When pressed to talk about his work, Leo revealed he assists disabled people with their trips to Peru in the low season. That is the good thing about access to this mountainous country, there are still so many alternatives to choose. Each trip can be as difficult or as easy as you wish to make it; they are prepared to cater for all our needs. Leo added that he makes most of his money in the high season, just enough to look after his family for the year, but with little else to spare. He didn't add anything about tips, but they obviously are important to his annual salary. He really comes across as a caring, non-assuming person; we were lucky to have him as our guide.

As there were trees and bushes lining our trail today we were advised to make use of our mosquito repellent. Prior to beginning this trip we were given a list of items to bring with us, so this requirement came as no surprise. The horses would also get a covering, which was something I hadn't considered. I suppose in the wild they just had to put up with the discomfort, so a positive tick in the box for mankind's intervention on this occasion. I also began to use some sunscreen, as the back of my neck was showing signs of colouring (another potential ailment then!).

At our usual departure time of 08:30 we found the four members of the lodge staff lined up outside to say their goodbyes. When these niceties had been completed we mounted our horses, turned our backs to the lodge and slowly headed out west along the trail. Colpa Lodge was a mere four-hour ride away, which we would no doubt cover with ease.

The mountainsides were now full of forests of dark green trees, as complete a contrast to the first few days as it was possible to imagine. On one side we had the safety of the mountain, while on the other the undergrowth was somewhat masking the dangers below. I knew a fall would still be very serious, but somehow it didn't look as bad with the dense foliage to break my fall. While Caesar and I were coping quite well, I spared another thought for the hikers. Their route may have been different, but with another day under their belts they surely must be starting to feel the strain.

We were now encountering lots of twisting, turning, narrow paths, with very small stones underfoot. If the paths were on level ground this would have been a straightforward enough operation; all I would have to consider was when to begin the turn. But as I was also descending (for the most part anyway), I had to once again adjust my position in the saddle. Leaning back was OK, but it meant I soon ran out of rein; at times I only had enough to hold in my fingertips. If they were any shorter I would have lost them altogether, which would have been disastrous. At least during these manoeuvres we were going slowly enough that I didn't have to worry about rising and falling in the saddle as well.

We stopped, after nearly two hours, at Rayanpata (3,388m) to rest the horses. We were protected from the sun by an avenue of overhanging trees lining our path. Here the horses got their top-up of mosquito spray, the humans too. If it wasn't for these buzzing insects around us it would have been quite a pleasant environment. This was certainly the better side of the mountain range to live on and, to emphasise that point, we were now seeing wooden-panelled, thatched roofed houses sporadically lining our route. If further proof were needed that we were indeed re-entering the civilised world, we were soon joined by a friendly dog, although the owner was nowhere in sight.

Before setting off we had to wait for yet another mule train to trot by; I was still amazed by their stamina. In some ways they remind me of the soldiers from the east marching in formation, their stride exaggerated with high kicking motions. It's hypnotic and mesmerizingly tragic to watch humans and animals perform to this type of tune. It was hard to tell if these particular mules were carrying our luggage as the contents were housed in large orange-coloured bags. If they were, then given their number, they would have been carrying about forty kilogrammes each which sounded about right, although I wouldn't have liked to carry that amount.

We continued on for another hour before our next stop at a local campsite. Leo led us up some rickety stairs to the upper part of a large wooden structure, while Oscar and Isaial tended the horses. There we found a seating area and a balcony offering a panoramic view of the site. The corrugated tin roof above our heads must have sounded amazing when it rained, but I was content enough with the weather as it was. Leo then disappeared for a few minutes, but soon returned rather pleasingly carrying a large bottle of Pilsen lager for us to share. We had proper glasses too, a genuine treat both well received and deserved. There is nothing like the fresh air, hot sun (with shade) and a lengthy horse ride, but a glass of beer was the cherry on top of the icing on the cake.

From my viewpoint I could see individual, open-faced straw wigwams sited around the perimeter of the camp. These shelters were there to offer additional protection from the weather to the tents pitched within. There were no signs of any backpackers at this time, but I didn't envy them at all if this was the choice they made, despite the good beer. I do like to try different things, but I am at the stage in my life where I prefer a little comfort. Maybe a stay in a nice hotel or even a well-built lodge serves my purpose better.

While we sat in the shade, drinking cold beer, our friends the hikers appeared and lined up for a zip wire ride. I watched as they wearily took off their daypacks and stood in the hot sun receiving safety and operational instructions. They were too far away for me to offer them refreshment and most looked like they desperately needed something cold and alcoholic. My earlier curiosity about how they were faring was now answered without them needing to comment. They were all a little older than me, but age is not always the best indicator, as fitness levels and inner desire also play a huge part in adventures of this nature. As they were traversing the valley, I now expected them to arrive at the lodge before us today, which would be a first for this trip. Our route would now force us to go down, back up and around the valley.

It was a real wrench to leave our temporary sanctuary; I could have sat there all day, drinking ice-cold beer in the shade. But, as we had our horses to think of, not to mention lunch and the promise of a refreshing shower waiting for us, Leo got us up and moved us on.

A few kilometres out from the Colpa Lodge (2,870m) we encountered a flat, wide-open plain. This was the cue for the lead horses to break into a canter and run for home and Caesar was not going to be left behind. As soon as the other horses set off I felt Caesar surge forward on the reins before slightly hesitating. Without question he wanted to run, but he wasn't quite sure how I would react. When I leaned forward and urged him on, he really broke into his full stride and kept pace with the others. The power exuding from his body was absolutely incredible and I could tell he was really enjoying stretching his legs. For my part I found the ride both exhilarating and terrifying in equal measure. As a novice I had never travelled at anything like this speed before.

Oscar occasionally glanced over his shoulder to see how I was coping, but as I was managing well enough, he continued to push on. This wasn't quite a 'wind in the hair' experience, due to my riding helmet, but nevertheless it was truly amazing. The only issue I had was finding somewhere to hold on to, and I really did need to hold on with more than just my legs. I had not given it much thought up to now, which wasn't too clever of me. The reins were now useless as they were just too flexible, so I grabbed hold of the front of the saddle for dear life. I knew if I became unbalanced by leaning too far back or even upright I would undoubtedly fall off.

As we rode on I managed to keep rising and falling in tune with Caesar's rhythm – in fact I was surprised to learn it was actually easier at this speed to be at one with the horse. As we neared the lodge I felt my vice-like grip on the saddle begin to weaken and I knew I would not have the opportunity to release and make adjustments. I also knew if I fell at this stage I would do myself some serious harm. Bones would be broken at the very least and that would be the end of my trip. I might also receive a kicking from the horse (and probably from Oscar as well). Fortunately, as we drew near to the lodge, we encountered a natural upward slope. Coupled with Oscar's zigzagging in front I managed to slow sufficiently to regain control, not to mention my composure. My legs felt like jelly when I dismounted, and it took a while for the exhilaration to wear off.

With the euphoria of the ride still fresh in my mind I then made a small error of judgement in terms of timing.

We had been advised that our lunch today would be buffet style and cooked in an open fire pit outside the lodge. As the hikers had surprisingly not yet arrived I thought I had time for a quick shower and change of clothing before the demonstration. Even though I was back in less than ten minutes, the hikers had arrived and the chefs had the food all wrapped, buried and covered with hot stones and earth.

I picked up a bottle of Cusquena Negra from the bar and returned outside once more, ensuring I would at least be there for the unveiling. I found the dark beer a bit too sweet for my liking, so I wasn't having a good afternoon. As I waited, Leo approached me and handed over my plastic pocket watch. I had only just noticed it was missing and thought it was lost forever. It seemed during the canter it had slipped out of my pocket. Oscar had somehow seen it fall, presumably when he had glanced back to see if I was OK, and had gone back over a kilometre to retrieve it. It had very little financial or sentimental value, but I was glad to have it returned as I still had times to adhere to and I don't wear a watch.

After nearly half an hour had elapsed helpers arrived to uncover the buried package. It took them a few minutes to remove the earth with their shovels to expose a heavy-duty blue sheet. Once this was pulled to one side they removed the hot stones to reveal several different types of potatoes, which was a little underwhelming. It seemed I hadn't missed too much after all. I had been expecting to at least see some meat, as it did seem a lot of work for such a simple staple. Once fully uncovered the potatoes were then transferred to large stainless-steel trays and transported to the kitchen.

As we adjourned inside, one of the guides brought out the meal's main attraction...a whole cooked cuy. He explained that the vermin were only eaten on special occasions, but I don't think anyone heard much of what he was saying. The expression on the animal's face was alarming to say the least; it appeared to be making a silent scream. I thought back to the cute little animals I saw a few days ago running around in the restaurants shed. The fluffy coat had long since disappeared and it now took on the appearance of a rat, albeit without the long tail. The skin was tight and shiny, almost as if someone had varnished it. In some ways it reminded me of Peking duck, the type that is hung up in Chinese restaurant windows for days on end. This was quite a spectacle and the next time we would see it would be when it was chopped up and put on the buffet table. At least we had a choice of whether to try a piece or not.

When I looked over at the buffet table I could see we had quite a good spread before us. There were all the usual types of fare: salad, a mixture of dips, cold sliced meats, at least four different types of potatoes, chicken...guinea pig. The main issue I had with the presence of a cooked rodent on our dinner table was its presentation. As I have mentioned earlier I don't like seeing an animal displayed in its natural, distinguishable form. This creature and several more of its kind, judging by the quantity, had not been sliced or diced; they were just quartered and presented simply on a plate with the rest of the meats. I tentatively took the least offensive looking piece, which to my mind was the front quarter with a scrawny leg attached. Once seated, I lifted it to my mouth and took a bite, ensuring Melanie photographed the occasion for posterity.

I have tried many times to explain the taste to people, without too much success. First of all, the skin is impossibly chewy and tasteless, like shoe leather (I would imagine), so I abandoned that. Then there was the flesh; I first tried a piece just under the skin, which was very thin and very fatty. I found the only way to remove a piece was to scrape it off with my teeth. I would describe it as 'savoury'. I had expected to tell people it was like chicken – that's the normal flavour for something different, isn't it – or like pork, but it simply wasn't. It had a taste all of its own. The inner part was even harder to describe as they had stuffed it with a pungent green vegetable which completely overpowered the taste.

One of the younger guides confided in us that although he is occasionally presented with a cuy when he returns home, he is not a big fan. He dutifully eats it, but only to please his elders. I think in this case the Peruvians are trying a little too desperately to hang on to their past. I accept they are not alone in this regard; there are many nations who consume the most unpalatable of things. The Scots eat haggis, the Koreans eat dogs, the French eat snails and the Australians drink Fosters.

To sum up my thoughts on the meal…I really liked the potatoes; I would try them all again, they were all slightly different in their way. The chicken and other accompaniments were all fine, which came as no surprise. But, in a message to all the Peruvians around the world, if you have to do your food shopping in a pet shop, then something is seriously wrong with your diet. With lunch out of the way I now had several hours to relax before dinner, where hopefully there would be no sign of rodents on the menu.

At 16:00 I took up Leo's offer of an escorted walk around the adjacent man-made orchid forest. Now it may not come as a complete surprise to you, but I wouldn't really describe myself as a keen botanist. However, there was nothing else to do and out of a sense of loyalty to Leo I went along. Before we entered the small forest Leo began his talk by revealing that, as well as having a social policy involving the locals, his company also had an environmental policy. This included the cataloguing of species of plants and the formation of orchid nurseries. They also compost and, among many other things, limit the use of plastic bottles by using water machines in the lodges. The stainless-steel drinking bottles Leo presented at our first meeting were a testament to this type of commitment.

I was accompanied on the tour by Melanie and Amy who were very keen to view orchids in the wild. Leo led the way, occasionally identifying the different species by their Latin names, which I could only assume were correct. The orchids I discovered were smaller than my fingernail, which came as a surprise as I thought they were going to be the size of my fist or bigger. Maybe I have mixed them up with another type of flower? What I found more interesting about the walk, though, was the complete absence of biting, crawly things. I came fearing the worse and I decided if I did get bitten then I only had myself to blame; I even had an exit strategy if things got too bad. But this was the weirdest wood I have ever visited; there simply weren't any insects to be seen or heard. We continued slowly winding our way along the twisting, turning trail for an hour until we eventually emerged from the other end.

Just before dinner the staff surprised the group by dressing up and acting out a traditional play for our amusement. We were first alerted to their arrival by the commencement of loud fiesta-style music, piped into the room via some sort of portable music device. The staff then leapt into the bar/dining area wearing face masks (which had previously been hanging on the wall) and colourful costumes. The derogatory storyline seemed to concern a Spanish tax inspector with an enormous, unflattering nose. After the initial dance the performers then randomly selected individuals to join them for round two. This culminated with the whole group joining hands and dancing energetically around the dinner table. It was quite a surreal experience and we got to forget we were adults for a while. Their enthusiasm was infectious and it was just a bit of fun after all, but given our efforts over the last few days, did they really think we were not getting enough exercise as it was?

After dinner the hikers had their own Pisco sour lesson, while those not involved sat and relaxed near the fire. Unfortunately though, they made too much of the mixture and invited Melanie and I to join them in a toast. This rather unexpected development meant I had to endure another glass of that wonderful drink.

Galloping horses, guinea pig for lunch, Pisco sour at the bar – only in Peru…what a day!

CHAPTER TEN

Journey to Lucma Lodge

After yesterday failing to find a single insect in the orchid garden, I woke at 02:30 to find a group of ten mosquito bites on my left thigh. Either they were the stealthiest creatures known to man or the reason they were absent from the forest was now clear…they were all residing in my bedroom. I shall now have a well-deserved rant about these despicable creatures.

Mosquitos exist solely to be part of the food chain and nothing more and that's a fact. But they aren't even good at that as their predators would quite easily find alternative sources of nourishment if they ceased to exist. They offer nothing to the world and irritate everyone they come into contact with; they are like traffic wardens. The parasites steal our blood while we sleep (mosquitos, not traffic wardens), which I wouldn't mind too much as I have plenty to spare, but they have to leave that itchy spot behind when they are finished. They also carry life-threatening diseases like dengue fever and the Zika virus. This latest development has led scientists in the United States to take a selection of them and genetically alter their reproductive system. When released back into the environment it is hoped that the modifications will decimate their numbers. Well good riddance, I say!

Breakfast was at an earlier time of 07:00 today as Leo had arranged for us to dine with the porters before they set off with our luggage. These men really had a thankless job guiding the heavily laden mules from lodge to lodge, an oversight that we would rectify this morning. The route they travel along is dusty, often dangerous and is repeated on a daily basis. It must also be quite disturbing when one of their mules falls off the mountain. As well as witnessing the accident, which is bad enough, they then have to deal with the aftermath. As they couldn't simply abandon their cargo, they would have to climb down and retrieve the items.

Despite Leo's best endeavours this morning, the porters failed to show up, so we dined alone once more. They missed out on scrambled eggs and crispy bacon, as well as the prospect of one last round of tips and some appreciation.

We left base at the usual time of 08:30 with the realisation that we were to say goodbye to the horses in a few hours' time. Despite the discomforts, and genuinely scary moments, I was really glad I chose the riding option. I was to walk tomorrow and although I was pleased to do so, the prospect didn't fill me with the same enthusiasm. The only worry I did have about today's journey concerned Leo's statement during last night's briefing. He had informed us that we were to canter for 'a while', but had left it at that. I had agreed, as I didn't want to hold the others back, particularly Melanie, but I must admit to feeling a little apprehensive. Yesterday's sprint finish had been amazing, without question and I now understand the attraction of riding these powerful beasts. However, the more times you try these dangerous activities, the more chances there are of something going seriously wrong.

Isaial led the way once more on foot, as we crossed bridges and forded streams, cutting corners whenever he could. He was scampering around like a mountain goat to keep up so he must have been really fit. Like yesterday, the trail was all tree and bush-lined, partially hiding the dangerous slopes from view. On one particularly narrow section I caught Caesar glancing down, over the edge, as we were so near. I saw fear in his eye so I pulled the reins sharply to turn his head away, forcing him to look straight ahead. I was worried enough for both of us; I didn't want him to panic and take us over the side.

I was slowly beginning to notice the horse's individual personality traits – people have them so why not animals? This was painfully emphasised while the horses took on some water from one of the streams; without warning, Oscar's horse casually wandered over to me and purposefully head-butted me on the knee. No one else noticed, not even Oscar who was on board and had let the reins go slack for a moment. It really was quite an extraordinary incident; he was clearly targeting me and not Caesar.

Later, again while the other horses were drinking, Caesar got too close to another horse and got spooked, causing him to raise his front legs high in the air. This was more than a little disconcerting as we were very near the edge of the mountain. In the next few seconds several things then happened at once. Out of the corner of my eye I saw Oscar immediately set off towards me, fearing the worst. Instinctively I held on to the reins and as Caesar landed back on four legs I immediately wheeled him away to the right, while simultaneously patting him on the left side of his neck, leaning forward and adding some reassuring words. To my amazement the situation ended as quickly as it began and before Oscar got even halfway to me.

Our first rest stop was at 10:00 where I spotted twenty-three baby ducklings (I counted them) waddling around in an adjacent, grassy garden. These creatures were certainly free-range, but it looked a bit careless of the absentee owner to allow them this sort of freedom without any protection whatsoever. Any wandering predator would have had easy pickings, and a tasty snack they looked too.

Our second rest stop at 11:30 was at the El Mirador campsite where I took some pictures of plastic lizards that were lying about. I planned to show them to the Americans to test both their knowledge of foreign wildlife and sense of humour. The first was wedged firmly in a bush and blended into its surroundings quite well. I expected more trouble convincing them about the Tyrannosaurus Rex as it wasn't as well camouflaged.

I hadn't expected to come across large purpose built campsites along this route. I had expected these unfortunates to be pitching their tents in the middle of nowhere, huddling together each night around a campfire for warmth. What I hadn't expected to find was structured facilities for washing, eating and drinking. Although I didn't see what could be described as a bar, I knew there was alcohol available, which is a symbol of civilisation in itself.

Our third stop was at a local cantina where I chatted with some young Australians; now they do like to travel. Aussies and Kiwis are like Irish bars and McDonald's outlets, it is virtually impossible to travel the world without encountering them. The Aussies' rite of passage no doubt stems from something inside, deep-rooted in their make-up, a legacy left behind by their ancestors, no doubt. It was a long way to travel from England all those years ago, made particularly uncomfortable with the chains weighing them down. Today they may be trying to find their way back 'home'; when I encounter them I don't let on that I know the way.

I think this group looked upon the horses with a little envy, certainly curiosity and possibly even a little admiration at the riders for choosing the option. When it was time to depart, I casually mounted up, swung Caesar around and rode off quickly behind the others. The manoeuvres were all expertly conducted in one motion of course and Caesar played his part…if only they knew.

As we were now encountering these campsites on a regular basis it was obvious we had arrived at the point where the Salkantay trail joined the final part of the Inca trail. When comparing the two routes I initially favoured the Salkantay version, despite the altitude issues, because of the peace and quiet. But now I look back I think it would have been interesting to join these other groups, as there seemed to be an unspoken camaraderie in the air. No one complained about the hardship because they were all experiencing it, they were all in it together; these trails are two sides of the same coin.

Today, more than any other, also re-enforced a belief I had since I first entered the mountains. Walking or riding these trails to Machu Picchu was what it was all about. The experience of several days off the beaten track, firstly at one with nature, then secondly meeting new people, is something I will always remember.

My contemplative musings came crashing back down to earth shortly after leaving this last campsite. The trail was now littered with plastic bottles and crisp packets, which was so out of place in this lovely environment and truly bewildering to see. Everyone would be carrying a daypack of some description and the items of packaging would weigh less now they were empty, so what's the problem with taking them with you? This situation reminds me of the motto of the Baltimore Grotto Caving Society which I first saw in China, while approaching one of the Great Walls:

'Take nothing but photos'
'Leave nothing but footprints'
'Kill nothing but time'

Soon after setting off I managed to briefly get lost in an orchard, which really took some doing. There were lots of twists and turns to the path and Caesar was in one of his lazy moods, just ambling along, falling behind again. I soon reached a fork in the trail and as the trees temporarily hid the others from view, I had to decide whether to go left or right. I could have called out, as I knew the others were not that far ahead, but instead I just opted to go left. If I was wrong I was sure to find out very soon and correct the mistake. Caesar had other ideas though; upon feeling my guidance to go to the left, he pulled the reins out of my hands and went to the right. Around the bend I found the team embarking on another steep twisting climb, oblivious to my plight. My companion had either remembered the way or had heard or sensed the other horses. However he had managed it, I had been put in my place and I now felt more like a passenger on Caesar's trip over the mountain.

Given the time of day, I sensed we were coming to the end of the ride and we were yet to break into anything other than a fast trot. So, while the horses stopped to take on water, I beckoned Oscar over to adjust my stirrups. I had allowed them to be loosened this morning without complaint, as it lessened the pressure on my knees. But they were slightly too long, and I had already slipped out of them on a number of occasions. With the canter to come I needed something to push down on and to raise myself out of the saddle, otherwise I would just be bouncing along and Caesar would justifiably want to throw me off.

Within a few minutes of the adjustment we did indeed embark on one last exhilarating gallop. Like yesterday the other horses set off first before Caesar's powerful body suddenly lunged forward beneath me. That initial surge is the best part – it is like a jet liner on take-off – but it is also the worst time for a beginner. If you anticipate it and have a firm grip on the saddle when it occurs, then the chances are that everything that follows will be fine. If you are unprepared, then you and the horse will soon be parted, and most uncomfortably.

As Caesar worked his way up through the gears, I just hung on for all I was worth. The wind, which had been sadly lacking all day, was now blowing strongly against my face and it felt great. The power these horses display, when allowed to run this freely, is amazing to behold, but this is also tempered by a degree of recklessness. The short sun-bleached, wispy grass had many a small hole and stone hidden within, just waiting for Caesar to inadvertently find and stumble upon. I knew that he wouldn't have cared less if I had fallen off, but he also placed his own safety secondary to his desire to run as fast as he could. Enjoyable as this no doubt was for him, it may also have led to broken bones and possibly his own demise.

I was pleased we kept up with the others, as I have my pride. I cannot imagine how people manage to go any faster; this really was fast enough given these ground conditions were far from ideal. My knees took one last battering before Oscar decided it was time we slowed and with no slope to assist, he had only his zigzagging technique to rely upon. It took a little longer by this method alone, but when we had slowed sufficiently I was once again able to assist by reining Caesar in. When we eventually came to a stop I gave him one last congratulatory pat on the left side of his neck (Caesar, not Oscar, although it would have been equally justified).

I will accept that horse riding isn't for everyone, but on this trip I took a chance and it paid off handsomely. I am now of the opinion that horses really are magnificent creatures and far more intelligent than I had first given them credit for. Caesar was conditioned to serve novices such as myself and he carried out his duties impeccably. I am still amazed by how easy he was to manoeuvre around the often tricky terrain.

If I were to ride again it would have to be as part of a similar trip. I know there must be other treks that provide a similar programme, but the journey or final destination must be worth all the pain and sores. To this end I have briefly carried out some post-trip research, but I have yet to find a dedicated horse trek that appeals. Most are just short-duration additions to longer tours. One or two hours, over the course of a week, really doesn't compare to a five-day ride over the Andes.

We were unable to reach the final lodge on horseback as the approach was through a steep, wooded incline. Having been pre-warned about the short hike I had packed my hiking boots in my saddlebags. As I changed my footwear I discreetly sorted out some money for Oscar and Isaial. They were to turn around immediately and start the long journey home, presumably travelling while the light was still good.

After the goodbyes and tips were dispensed, Leo led us up the first part of the trail. As Melanie was still wearing her smooth-soled riding boots she struggled a little with the terrain. Leo had to occasionally drop back to assist, while I continued on at a much-reduced pace until they caught up. I found it preferable to trudge slowly on, with my head down, rather than keep stopping and starting every five minutes. I soon came upon a fork in the trail and stopped to wait for Leo's guidance. But before he caught up, the hikers unexpectedly appeared from another path and took the low road. I reasonably assumed we were all heading for the lodge so I tucked in behind the last person. It was only when Leo called to me I realised I should have stayed on the upper path. The hikers were on their way down to visit a coffee harvesting business. Our visit was scheduled for later on today, when the temperature was a little cooler and we were well rested.

I later learned that the hikers had to be driven for part of the way today, as their route was under repair and unsafe to traverse, which explained their early arrival. This development would have annoyed me somewhat because it would have made the journey seem incomplete somehow. I may also have had trouble getting Caesar into the boot of the car.

Overall it took half an hour to ascend this steep wooded incline and it wasn't the most pleasant of experiences, due to the insufferable heat and humidity; I could have also done without my earlier impromptu diversion. It was just before 13:00 when we emerged through the trees and finally came upon Lucma Lodge (2,150m), which was set in a most picturesque location. It appeared to be built into the side of the mountain, surrounded as it was by trees and bushes. All the other lodges had been located in the middle of vast plains in between the mountains. Here was a jungle lodge, similar in design, but more at one with nature.

The staff greeted us with a welcome, cold towels and papaya juice drinks. The fruit juice was refreshing, but after a quick shower it was straight to the bar for a proper drink. As the member of staff was a little unsure about the selection available, I escorted her into the kitchen, checked out the fridge and chose my favourite bottle of dark Erdinger. I found the staff at every lodge very helpful, but sometimes you have to take charge, particularly when alcohol is involved.

I think we sometimes forget that young people often sell drinks they have never tried for themselves. There weren't any issues in any of the lodges as my needs were limited to a cold beer, but in the past I have numerous examples of bar staff in English pubs not quite getting it right. I once asked for single whisky and lemonade, only to receive the spirit at my table drowned in half a pint of lemonade. Gin and tonic should have a small measure of tonic water added before passing the rest of the bottle to the customer so they can adjust to taste for themselves. Lager top should have a splash of lemonade in the TOP where the sweet concentration will linger…I could go on. When Leo appeared, I bought him a drink and he chose the dark Erdinger as well – great minds think alike.

We had a surprise when we sat down to lunch – one might almost say a shock – as there was no soup! It had been on the menu for every lunch and dinner so far, but as we were now at a lower altitude and not suffering from dehydration effects, we were presumably free to try other dishes. Our starter today then was a mixture of beans, banana, melon, red onion and an assortment of other chopped up items. I could be a little cynical and say they were getting rid of the leftovers. The main course was visually less appealing, as it looked like an attempt at chicken supreme, while looking anything but supreme; to be fair it actually tasted a lot better than it looked. The meal was completed by a dessert of chopped fruit salad, similar in appearance and construction to the starter.

After lunch I relaxed in the common room, browsing through the magazines about Peru. Without a fire I soon got cold and retired to my room, mainly to get some warmth from my propane heater, but also to have a lie-down.

At 17:00 I met up with Leo and Melanie for our visit to the coffee business. I could see from the lodge that a light and misty rain had descended so I brought my thin black poncho with me. After days of being prepared for rain I finally had reason to use my wet-weather gear. Although the weather was less favourable than when we first arrived, it was now significantly cooler and we were well rested. Leo had definitely made the right decision to book us in for the late afternoon session.

Along the way Leo pointed out the coffee beans growing on nearby bushes; some were green, others red. If I were journeying through this wood alone I would have overlooked them, mistaking them for common berries. I also spotted a wild pineapple growing on the floor in the centre of a nest of metre-long thin leaves. I had never seen a pineapple growing in the wild before; it looked so out of place among the leaves, as if someone had placed it there as a joke.

Upon arrival we quickly established that the owner did not speak English, so Leo described the process as we progressed through the different stages. We were told that the staff had picked some beans earlier in the day and laid them out in the sun to dry out. They were ready for collection when they had turned white and were completely devoid of moisture. Now the owner took some of these dried beans and placed them in the roasting oven. Leo assisted by operating the bellows, while she vigorously stirred the pot.

After roasting, the beans were placed into a sieve to remove the loose outer husks. Nothing was wasted however, as this residue would be sent to the producers of inferior, but popular, coffee brands which adorn our supermarket shelves back home. The whole roasted beans were then transferred into a stainless-steel hand grinder. Melanie and I were invited to take turns rotating the handle until all the contents were reduced to a rich powder. Some of this powder was then placed into a perforated jar that sat atop a white china coffee pot; hot water was then added to the mix. We then waited until the coffee filtered through and we had enough of the liquid to sample.

As expected, it had that unmistakeably bitter taste of real coffee and was very good. It had been interesting to watch those coloured beans transform into a familiar drink. It made me wonder how someone discovered that by burning and grinding up some dried beans from neighbouring bushes it would lead to a tasty drink. We were inevitably invited to buy some of the roasted produce in large packets, but I declined. I couldn't be bothered to transport it around the country and as good as it was I could surely find the equivalent back home if I so desired.

After enjoying a few mouthfuls of the hot beverage, the owner brought a white plastic bottle over to the table. I am not sure what it was, as it had no label, but like the coffee it was definitely homemade (and alcoholic). I thought I would give it a try, for research and medicinal purposes. As I tilted the bottle forward, nothing came out of the opening; I gently angled it a little further until, all of a sudden there was a flood of liquid. I now had more hooch than coffee, so I had to discreetly return to the coffee pot for a top-up – a genuine mistake due to the shape of the bottle. It warmed me through quite nicely and I could have stayed for a while longer, but with our session completed it was time to head back to the lodge.

Outside, in the semi-darkness, Leo pointed to some trees where chickens were sleeping in the branches, and that wasn't the alcohol affecting my vision. They apparently do this to keep out of the reaches of predators; I bet the locals eat a lot of omelettes and scrambled eggs. This was as strange a sight to see as the pineapple earlier. I was beginning to feel like I was in another world, with all the things I thought I knew about nature now turned on their head.

The slight upward ascent through the wood was a little tricky in the gloom. The fine rain had made the floor very slippery and I had to watch my step to avoid the tree roots and equally slippery mulched-up leaves. At the same time there were head-height tree branches to avoid. I didn't realise at the time, but this was a small sample of what I would face during tomorrow's hike.

We arrived back at the lodge just after 18:00 to find everyone watching a BBC documentary about an Inca dig expedition. I noted their guide hadn't waited for us to return before he started the video. The programme reflected our trip in some ways, as the archaeological site was way up in the mountains. Watching the Norwegian-led team struggling to battle through the snow-covered terrain was interesting; I shared their pain. But in terms of achievement the expedition failed to deliver, as they ran out of time before they found anything of significance. The film passed the hour until dinner, which aside from tomorrow's breakfast, was to be our last meal prepared by the chefs. Soup was back on the menu with noodles on this occasion, followed by a dish with beef, mashed potato and vegetables, completed unsurprisingly by coffee-flavoured ice cream.

After dinner I settled my multi-lodge tab (just a few beers and the one unforgettable massage) before sitting down with Leo and Melanie. Tonight's meeting was a little different as Leo had two options for us to consider for tomorrow. We could either join the main group for the full day's hiking or go on a half-day canopy zip-wire tour, both with lunch included along the way. The multi-zip-wire tour was definitely Melanie's preference, but the booking would require at least two people. Given her lack of alternative footwear I don't think she had intended to do any hiking.

This put me under a bit of pressure, but I was now set on joining the others walking the trail; I had yet to experience any real hiking and didn't want to go home without spending at least one day on the Inca trail. I also felt it would be good to arrive at our destination as a group. In truth though, I would have liked to have taken up both options. If we were staying at this lodge for another day I would have gladly joined Melanie, as the views would have been amazing. Despite not particularly liking heights I would have still gone, for I would have valued the experience above all else.

Melanie tried on several occasions to change my mind, not in a forceful way, more in desperation than anything else, but I was not going to be swayed. If I were in her position, I would have offered to pay for one of the staff to come with me. If there were no takers, I would have offered to pay double for just myself; the owners would surely have allowed that, as they only want their money. We had spent thousands of pounds on this trip, so for me to spend a couple of hundred pounds more (on something I desperately wanted to do) would have made little difference. Without managing to secure the necessary second person, Melanie had no other option but to join me and the others on the hike over the last mountain. Machu Picchu lay beyond.

CHAPTER ELEVEN

Aguas Calientes

Last night I gave my generous tip to Leo and bade him farewell, which was a little sad (the saying goodbye part, not the handing over of the money). He had really looked after me and was a most genuine and likeable person, but all good things must come to an end. Whilder and Claudio would continue to lead the hiking team, of which the ex-horse riders were now part. This morning, instead of making our way to another lodge, we were headed to the remote train station at La Hidroelectrica. The train would take us to the town of Aguas Calientes, where our new accommodation awaited.

Breakfast was at an unbelievably early time of 06:00 as we had to leave by 07:00 if we were to keep to our schedule. I actually had a goodnight's sleep for the first time in living memory and I needed it because the hike was scheduled to take between six and seven hours, depending on the pace set by our guides. I was actually looking forward to hiking this morning, despite never having walked such a long distance before.

Now firmly on the ground, I would be looking at my surroundings from a new perspective. I could stop whenever I wanted to take photos or even to catch my breath, if I felt the need. When I reached the train station the arrival would mark the end of the long trail through the mountains.

Before we departed we also had to say goodbye to the chefs, as all our meals would now be taken care of by others. The food they prepared on the trail had been satisfactory – not exactly what I would call fine dining, but acceptable enough. I particularly liked the spicy, finely chopped salsas I added as a condiment to the omnipresent soup. The main courses were a little hit and miss; without being too critical, they sometimes lacked a little on the presentation side. In terms of the variety though, I had no issues whatsoever, which is important to me.

Once assembled outside it was decided that Alberto would make a thank-you speech on our behalf, and in the chef's native Spanish, before handing over our combined envelope of tips. It was soon apparent that he wasn't a fluent Spanish speaker. I had no idea what was being said, but then I wasn't totally convinced that he knew either. But I was sure the chefs got the meaning of what we were trying to say and that was the main thing.

As we were about to set off I looked around and noticed everyone was carrying walking poles. It was then I remembered that I had left mine in Cusco, along with my excess luggage. I seem to remember during the packing process I actually decided not to bring them, which now seemed a ridiculous decision, given I had actually brought them to Peru for this express purpose. Tiredness and altitude sickness were to blame again, making my head a little muddled, both pre- and post-medication. I just hoped my hiking boots would prove to be sufficient; if they weren't I would be in for an uncomfortable day. Melanie was in an even worse situation, given her choice of footwear, but she had opted to borrow a long bamboo pole from the large selection at the lodge. As it looked a bit too cumbersome I still decided to go on without; I already had my daypack to carry and that was enough for me. I think we both were already missing our four-legged taxis; it seemed strange heading off without them. Our blue holdalls were once again spirited away and we would be reunited with them at the train station.

We left the lodge with Claudio leading the way and setting a reasonable pace, while Whilder rounded up the stragglers like me at the back. As a precaution I had ensured my arms, legs and head were covered, but once again I struggled to see or hear any insects along our jungle trail. It seemed my little companions from yesterday had remained behind in my room to await the next unfortunate guest.

As we set off there was plenty of cloud cover, shielding us from the sun, so I had no need of sun cream just yet. I quickly discovered that the others were, for the most part, a lot fitter than I was. I had hoped the previous five days had taken something out of their stride, but this proved not to be the case. Amy in particular was skipping along like a mountain goat at times; if she ever wanted a job in Peru she could easily take over from Isaial. The rest of us looked forward to the regular rest stops, but none of them lasted longer than ten minutes.

After two hours we reached the summit of the mountain we were ascending. I had managed adequately without my poles so far, but it was a different story once we headed down the other side. The forest floor was littered with slippery leaves and smooth, gnarly roots. I slid a few times and had to catch hold of the nearest tree to avoid falling over. I was offered a pole by one of the others, which I politely refused. I wasn't going to have them struggle at my expense, particularly as they had the sense to come properly prepared.

Fortunately, it wasn't all steep climbs and plunging drops though; occasionally the trail levelled out and I could relax a little. At times it was quite a pleasant walk and although I occasionally showed signs of tiring, I was coping well enough. I made sure I took in the scenery when I wasn't staring at the floor, avoiding trip hazards. The early days of riding over the mountains, where there was little plant growth at all, were now a distant memory. I was now surrounded by greenery for as far as the eye could see – there were thousands upon thousands of trees and bushes wherever I looked.

Admittedly this beautiful view was occasionally spoiled by pylons and overhead power lines, but I suppose that is progress. The early pioneers wouldn't have had this issue, so they were one up on me there. I could also just make out the occasional path zigzagging its way up the adjacent mountain. I noted it was far too steep for horses; some parts must have had steps cut out as they looked near vertical.

Before long we reached the Llactapata Pass (2,736m) and some Inca ruins. Most of the buildings we saw were still overrun with undergrowth, so they were a little underwhelming if I am being honest. But the main purpose of this stop was the view it offered of Machu Picchu. The site was still some distance away across the valley on a different mountain range, but it heralded the achievement of my goal.

The Spanish conquistadores never found Machu Picchu, which was surprising to learn as it was in use right up to their arrival and therefore not covered in undergrowth or masked in any way. From this location it was difficult to make out with the naked eye, so the detail had to be viewed through binoculars, but I could still see enough to decide it warranted further investigation.

We spent some time having several team photos taken by the guides as we took turns handing over our cameras. I found this stop a bit of a tease as we were so close and yet still a day away from actually visiting the site. We were told that not everyone who travels on the Inca trail gets to see the site from this viewpoint as it does require a small detour.

At 10:30 we stopped for a very early lunch at the Llaqtapata Lodge, a rustic-looking stopover that essentially comprised a long dining room (containing one large table) and a small kitchen. If guests wanted to stay within the grounds overnight, there were charges of S/.5 to pitch a tent and S/.10 to use their shower. Out of curiosity I popped into the kitchen to see lunch being prepared. I did like the informal nature of this trip; there seemed to be nothing to hide. Today we had a starter of avocado, a main course of trout, lentils, rice, chips and salad, with tinned peaches to finish.

While we waited for our food to be served, the guides kept us busy by taking individual photos of us making star jumps in front of Machu Picchu. That was just what I needed really, using up the little energy I had left! The view was slightly closer than our previous stop, but once again all we could see were some stone terraces, with very few roofless buildings visible.

After lunch Amy discovered a very large dead beetle on the way back from the toilet. It almost filled the palm of her hand – it was so big. While it was an unnecessary reminder that we were now in the jungle, this was still the closest I came to seeing anything smaller than a dog. I wouldn't have liked to have spent an evening walking through this area, as the billions of insects must be nocturnal. In return for showing me the beetle I showed Amy the pictures of the (plastic) lizards I had found; Melanie looked on with an expression that implied she thought I was being a little juvenile (I was!). At 11:20 we were told to ready ourselves for the restart of our journey.

I could now see thick white clouds surrounding the peaks of the neighbouring mountains; a small river snaked its way through the valley far below. The foliage was so thick it masked any chance I had of seeing anything living down there on those unforgiving slopes. We soon faced a steep descent where I once again struggled to keep my balance. I had to consider in advance where the best place was to plant my feet, concentrating really hard on each downward step I took; I now knew how Caesar had felt, on a day to day basis. Step by slippery step I soldiered on, dancing around the tree roots that were now extremely prevalent. These trip hazards occasionally came to my rescue as they prevented me from sliding too far down the slick trail. My knees were now starting to ache as well, as I had to keep my legs tensed up for long periods and hadn't taken my glucosamine tablets.

The temperature was starting to rise and I now understood why we had left so early. There were several trains we could have caught throughout the afternoon, but departing later would have meant walking a lot of hard kilometres under the hot sun. On the one hand I was hoping it wasn't too much further as I was getting rather parched and continuing to tire. But at the same time I was enjoying the fresh air, views and grind of the challenge.

An hour later we reached the Aobamba River and more importantly the fifty-metre bridge that spanned it. The bridge was constructed of vertical rope supports, with horizontal planks of wood for a base; the sides were fenced in with a thin wire mesh. There was a bit of a mixture of materials then, with the mesh looking like a later addition.

We were advised to cross the bridge in ones and twos as it was apparently a little rickety. This was not something we wanted to hear, being fifty-metres above a fast-moving, shallow river, containing jagged rocks. Despite the danger, the guides invited us to go halfway across for a photo opportunity; we then had to return for our cameras before crossing for real. This made the crossing a long and drawn-out process, but the guides attempted to make it fun. The threat of sudden death somehow lost its meaning with their attempted levity, although I noted they waited for us all to go across first; no one even questioned that.

We were on the home stretch now; the terrain had thankfully flattened out and we even came upon a sign notifying us of the direction of Machu Picchu. It was here that Whilder booked us in at a control checkpoint, identified as 'sector Inti Watana'. I hadn't expected to find any authorities prior to our arrival at the train station but here they were…two people in a green corrugated hut. Train tracks had now appeared which we followed towards the La Hidroelectrica train station. As we neared the end of this leg of the journey huge piles of rubbish appeared on our right, which I took as a sign we were indeed back in the civilised world.

Upon our arrival we had one final climb to make…the steps up to the Inca Samana bar, where we had a reserved table waiting for us. Of course it couldn't have been at ground level; in the true tradition of the Incas it was quite unnecessarily elevated above the other buildings. I was really tired now and desperately thirsty. It was a struggle to climb the twenty or so steps up to the balcony. I placed one foot after another, step by step until I reached the top. Thankfully Whilder and Claudio had arranged for a prepaid round of drinks to be served upon our arrival and they were quickly dispensed. The hike had only been eleven to twelve kilometres, but that did not take into consideration the effort required due to the elevations, heat and jungle environment. We finished at 13:20, taking just over the six hours expected, but that had also included our short breaks, photo opportunities and lunch.

When I am asked about the highlight of this trip, I tell people to forget about Machu Picchu and the horse riding, it was consuming that first large bottle of Cusquena lager. The second bottle wasn't bad either, although I had to pay for that one. That first beer reminded me of the film *Ice Cold in Alex,* which was set against the backdrop of World War Two, starring John Mills, Harry Andrews, Anthony Quayle and Sylvia Sims. The four protagonists endured a perilous journey through the North Africa desert. After many hardships they arrived at a safe haven, gasping for a drink, and headed for the nearest bar. The resulting pour of that first drink into an ice-cold condensing glass, the anticipation and finally the consumption of the beer by John Mills, is one of the greatest scenes in cinematic history.

Here in Peru was my *Ice Cold in Alex* moment.

After our drinks were consumed we then had to say goodbye to Claudio, as we now only needed one guide and Whilder was the more senior member of staff. Melanie hadn't seen me discreetly tip Claudio so she gave him her tip from both of us. I overheard her whispering about the money, but I didn't let on, good luck to him if she gave him extra. I could have sat in that bar for another few hours and most of the next day, come to that, but we had a train to catch.

At 14:20 the train approached, and we were so close we could almost touch its roof while sitting at our table. Without waiting to be asked, we made our way down to the trackside. There was no platform to speak of, but we thankfully found our luggage waiting for us, just off to one side. The mules must have survived the various journeys then without falling off the mountains, which was probably the only thing that could have gone wrong. This would have been a terrible thing to happen. Imagine being told that your luggage was delayed, but everything was in hand; it would be sent along on the next train once they had scraped off the remnants of the mule.

As tired as I was, I jumped on to the train steps and started a chain to transfer each bag up to Whilder, who in turn had placed himself just inside the door to the carriage. Once the bags and passengers were on-board we departed for Aguas Calientes and our new temporary accommodation.

The Vistadome train was one of a number of trains people can catch from either Poroy near Cusco, or from Ollantaytambo in the Sacred Valley. Once here at La Hidroelectrica train station it is on to Aguas Calientes, the basecamp town at the bottom of Machu Picchu. Of course travelling by train would have meant missing out on this fantastic adventure, but at least it is an option for the less able-bodied.

I was really pleased with all the arrangements that had been made today. Not only was there a beer waiting for us at the end of the hike, the train was on time and our luggage was there waiting for us and easily found. The train departed on schedule at 14:50, leaving me to inwardly congratulate all the organisers for their administrative skills. I know from experience that there are a lot of things that can go wrong when trying to prepare a trip like this.

Once underway, the view from the train was magnificent. There were glass panels in the ceiling and large windows at every four-seater table. We trundled along at a leisurely pace, which allowed everyone to sit back, relax and take in the views. I was sat apart from the others due to the ticket numbering, but that wouldn't be for long.

The train followed the course of the meandering Urubamba River for most of the journey, although the water course disappeared from sight at regular intervals. Alongside the tracks there was a myriad of plants, the like of which I had never seen in terms of diversity. There were spindly trees, plants with enormous broad leaves, others with long and thin leaves. There were bushes with a smattering of small colourful flowers, others with none at all. The only common factor seemed to be the colour, the overall theme being the darkest green. Beyond the greenery in the foreground I could see the imposing mountains, valleys and the largest of the trees.

It suddenly dawned on me that I had managed to ride a horse along the trail, hike and travel by train. Nine months earlier I thought I had to choose between these three options. They each had their own merits and were enjoyable in their own way. Admittedly I hadn't tried the camping, but I did at least visit some of the campsites, so I could live with that!

After an hour we arrived at Aguas Calientes station and had to decant our luggage once more. This time we had to carry our bags a short distance to meet the hotel porters, who in turn would ensure they reached the hotel. Once again everything was in order and carried out with the minimum of fuss.

The town of Aguas Calientes was constructed solely with Machu Picchu in mind. In order to reach the main part of the town we first had to navigate our way through some market stalls. These had all the expected types of tourist merchandise and bric-a-brac, not too dissimilar to the market at Pisac I had visited during the Sacred Valley tour. The restaurants that lay beyond all served typical tourist fare; I noticed some even had cuy on the menu. But most importantly it was from here, tomorrow morning, that we would be catching the shuttle bus to the top of the mountain and the Machu Picchu sanctuary. This felt like yet another step, but I was getting ever closer to my goal.

Once we arrived at the Inkaterra Pueblo hotel there were forms to complete and one last briefing to attend. Those who had signed up to the extension day received their bus and Machu Picchu entrance tickets for day two.

This extra day may seem superfluous, but I like to think I am cautious, rather than pessimistic, when it comes to trips of this nature. By visiting all of the Seven Wonders of the World at least twice on each visit, I ensure, as best as I can, that my time isn't compromised by mistakes, on my part or others'. For the larger sites such as Machu Picchu this second day also allows me to divide the visit into two parts to make it a little easier on my legs. The briefing ended with the news that tomorrow we were to meet in reception for a 07:00 departure, another early rise for breakfast.

I would describe the hotel as a complex, rather than the expected one-building establishment. We had convened in the bar area of the main building that also held the reception. There was a separate restaurant building where we were to dine later that evening, which I recognised from the train as we pulled into the station. The sleeping quarters were located within numerous accommodation buildings, scattered almost at random along meandering pathways in a jungle-like environment. All the roofs were thatched and made to look like ancient Inca dwellings. As a whole the setting looked like a bird sanctuary with its winding paths, bushes, trees and water features.

Incidentally, water features are installed in public places to cool the surrounding air and not merely to please the eye. This type of effect was known about from as far back as Roman times.

This environment usually means mosquitos (yes, them again) are present, so I would have to take precautions. I would have liked to have had a mosquito net as they really do work. I had used one once while on a one-week detox holiday in Koh Samui (an island off the coast of Thailand). I was staying high up in a mountainous forest, surrounded by bushes. At night the noise of so many mosquitos in my room led me to repeatedly check they were indeed on the outside of the net. I woke the next morning pleasantly surprised to learn I hadn't received a single bite.

The stand-alone accommodation blocks were on two levels and of course my room had to be on the upper level. So, as well as the steps between the pathway's varying levels, I also had more stairs to climb when I reached the correct building. Oh, my poor knees! Once inside I decided to leave the unpacking and just have a brief rest.

Once sufficiently refreshed I headed out to explore the town. I really should have rested up for longer as I had a big two days ahead of me, but my curiosity got the better of me. We were to spend two nights here and I wanted to know if it was worth staying in the hotel after dinner, or if I had the option of going elsewhere. Although the complex looked pleasant enough, it also looked very quiet.

I had a good idea of what to expect of the town as I had viewed most of it as we walked to the hotel. There were two main streets, one directly in front as I left the hotel and stretching ahead of me for two hundred metres or so, another to my left on the other side of the train tracks running parallel. I would describe the areas as basic, more in keeping with Cusco, than Lima but somewhat less refined.

It didn't take long to finish my exploration, so I stopped off and had a small pizza and a much-needed bottle of water; I needed to be fully hydrated if I was going to have a drink tonight. I returned to my room after an hour, not having found what I would call a bar – plenty of restaurants selling food and drinks, but that was it. Upon my return I unpacked, which felt like somewhat of a novelty after the temporary stays at the lodges. After another rest I readied myself for dinner.

In the bar Lewis bought me a Pisco sour which was nice of him. Although I am still a little undecided about the drink, it does seem to get a little better after each tasting; maybe I should have tried harder to develop a liking for it. The food this evening promised to be a real treat, all chosen from a menu, and we had an actual wine list! I started with Uchu Ujumpi, a Peruvian dish consisting of a hot pepper stuffed with meat and vegetables. For the main course I chose Ajiaco, which may be described as beef medallions with cubed potatoes. Both were immersed in sauces of some description. The meal was washed down with a bottle of Chilean Merlot I bought and shared with Lewis and Jyl. I didn't bother with dessert. This was probably the best meal I had on the trip.

After dinner I did step out, as there seemed nothing else to do. There was no television and the lights in my room were of insufficient brightness to allow me to read without straining my eyes. Oh, and I also wanted a beer. I took a slow walk around the hotel grounds, noting that the signposts directing people to their rooms were now difficult to read in the gloom. As I neared the reception building I heard music which sounded like it was coming from outside the complex. I approached the security guard watching the hotel entrance and made some enquiries.

Following his directions, I crossed the footbridge spanning the small stream which separated the hotel from the town. I then took a right turn, as soon as I was able, and walked on until I came upon a large, open raised square. There I found the locals enjoying some sort of party, the nature of which was a mystery at that stage. I knew the Peruvians have a number of festivals and like to celebrate each one with great enthusiasm. I initially joined the crowd, watching from the perimeter until I saw some cases of beer being carried around the back. I then quickly set off after them and offered to buy a bottle, only to find the organiser would not take my money. It seemed I had inadvertently gate-crashed a wedding party and all the drinks were free. I only stayed for the one I was offered as I felt slightly embarrassed at the intrusion. But I was made to feel welcome; they are a very friendly people, the Peruvians.

After leaving the square I briefly explored the town again in search of other potential venues, but quickly conceded defeat, which was probably just as well. I really didn't need a hangover to spoil tomorrow's visit. Upon my return to the hotel I went straight to bed, hoping the small intake of alcohol would help to induce a good night's sleep.

I wasn't to know at that time, but over the next few days I was to be presented with a series of challenges – yes, let's call them challenges. Something always seems to go wrong with my trips no matter how hard I try to plan for every eventuality. On this occasion, I suppose I should be thankful that at least fate had saved them all up for the end of the trip.

CHAPTER TWELVE

Machu Picchu

After spending eleven days in Peru acclimatising, sightseeing and trekking over the Andes, the day had finally arrived for me to pay the first of two visits to Machu Picchu. If all went as planned today, the second visit would be a most relaxed affair. I could spend the day viewing the site from a new perspective and maybe find some less-walked areas. After checking my photos from today I would also be able to retake as many as necessary to ensure I had a most comprehensive collection.

Although I awoke at 04:30 I still skipped breakfast for the first time on this trip as I wasn't at all hungry. Eating three meals a day, and usually three courses for the lunch and dinner sessions, soon takes its toll. Oh, the hardship I had to endure on this trip! I was therefore the first to meet Whilder in reception, well before 07:00 to receive my packed lunch, entrance and bus tickets. I carefully stowed the tickets and food away in my daypack and waited for the others to arrive.

At last night's briefing Whilder informed us that although we were not permitted to take the food inside the sanctuary, there were storage facilities and toilets just outside the main entrance. We were allowed to exit up to three times on the same ticket; our passports would ensure it was the same person utilising the ticket upon re-entry. This sounded like a very organised and agreeable arrangement. Just imagine travelling all this way, only to have to leave the sanctuary after half an hour to use the toilet and not being allowed to return!

Once the group was fully assembled, the tickets and food distributed, it was time to head through the town to catch the bus up the mountain. After we departed the hotel grounds we headed halfway down the main street before turning left to climb the steps of the footbridge which crossed the railway tracks. This increased elevation gave us an aerial view of the queue for the buses. There were only two thousand five hundred people allowed into the sanctuary today, but it initially seemed that all of them were in the queue ahead of us. In reality it was probably only a few hundred, but it did look quite imposing.

I did find this development a little annoying as I felt we could have left a little earlier to avoid this situation. The first bus sets off at 05:30, with the sanctuary opening at 06:00; I can't imagine many people travelling at that hour and I had been awake and ready to go. As a departure time, 07:00 was probably considered to be quite reasonable for all the tour groups to leave their individual hotels. It was also an easy time to remember – the tour guides wouldn't ask people to meet up at 06:42 or 06:47. Our problem was that we were based the furthest away from the bus queue, meaning we inevitably arrived there later than everyone else who also departed at 07:00.

Fortunately there were twenty-five buses on hand to carry out the shuttle runs up and down the mountain. So, after my initial fears that we would be queuing for hours, we were actually ready for boarding after only forty minutes or so.

At the door to the bus stood an officious looking ticket inspector, busily scanning tickets with a handheld device prior to the passengers being allowed on board. Given the amount of people travelling to the sanctuary, it looked like she would be in for a very busy day. I was the last of our group to present my ticket and of course there just had to be a problem with it. We were travelling on the 24/05/16, but my bus ticket was dated 25/05/16. I hadn't thought to check so I was partly to blame, but then again I had no idea what the date was on a day to day basis. I usually rely on the television, newspapers or my laptop, but I had none of them here on this leg of the trip.

Whilder, who had remained by the door until we were all aboard, then had a long and meaningful discussion with the young lady. As the heated debate was in Spanish I cannot reveal what was said, but I had the feeling all was not well. For my part I had little choice but to wait to one side, a little bemused at the goings-on. The only person I could have shouted at (in English) was the person trying to assist me, so that would have been counter-productive. At one point, in a break in the argument, Whilder turned to me and almost accusingly suggested I had muddled things up and produced tomorrow's ticket! He must have been getting desperate. After many words had been exchanged I was finally let on board, but as the ticket was also to be used for my return journey I still had that slight feeling of anxiety.

Understandably, when I joined the rest of the group they all wanted to know what the problem was. When I explained the situation, we discovered that all of the tickets had the same date, so why I alone was stopped I shall never know! To make matters worse, when I checked the date on the bus ticket for tomorrow's visit I found it was also incorrect. We were travelling on the 24/05/16 and 25/05/16, but the tickets we were given were for the 25/05/16 and 26/05/16. As I had now used the ticket for the 25/05/16 (which would have been OK for tomorrow) I would have further problems to come. Are you still with me? But that was for another day; I was now on board and we were on our way up the mountain to the sanctuary.

Once across the Urubamba River we made our way up the spiralling Carretera Hiram Bingham road. The road was named after the North American explorer Hiram Bingham III, whose best-known achievement was undoubtedly revealing Machu Picchu to the world. In 1911 he was led to the overgrown site by some locals, after spending many days climbing over the difficult terrain. It was hard enough now, so I can only imagine what it was like back then, trekking through the dense undergrowth. The locals lived solitary lives on the mountains, so they really had little idea people would be interested in the ruins of their ancestors' lost city. That outlook quickly changed once money was offered for the possibility that there may be Inca trinkets lying within.

Hiram Bingham III was an interesting character, and in many ways. Born in 1875 in Honolulu, Hawaii, he taught history and politics at Yale and Harvard Universities. He discovered many Inca ruins and wrote papers about each of them. He even had time to rise to Lieutenant Colonel in the US Air Force, before finally becoming a senator. He died in 1956, aged eighty, having led, I think it fair to say, a most interesting life.

As the mountain was very steep, we had to drive up in a zigzag fashion; on average we travelled about four hundred metres to the southeast, before turning sharply to travel four hundred metres northwest. There were thirteen hairpin bends in all to navigate through, as we meandered our way slowly to the top. The only other traffic we encountered was the returning buses, as the road was built solely for the journey to Machu Picchu and the adjacent hotel. I had considered staying at the Belmond Sanctuary Lodge, but the cost of S/.4000 for just one night was a bit too high to justify paying, given the limited time I would be spending there.

At the top (2,430m) we disembarked and found ourselves standing outside the hotel, some thirty or forty metres from the site entrance; I hadn't realised it was that close. Looking towards the main entrance and bag-checking area, I could see Huayna Picchu (or Wayna Picchu as it is also known) looming in the background, but I could see nothing else of the site. This is the mountain which is most photographed behind Machu Picchu. Later that morning, we were scheduled to climb it; from here it looked a most imposing proposition.

I handed my daypack over the counter for an attendant to deposit into a locker and made my way to the turnstile entrance, where I joined another busy queue to have my ticket and passport checked. As I waited I viewed the details on my ticket and was relieved to find the date correct. However, I failed to notice (until after the trip) that it had my age noted down as fifty-seven; there were times over the last few days when I felt ten years older, but this was a bit much! Fortunately this blunder was not picked up by the serious looking ticket inspector, as he looked a little less forgiving than the bus attendant. Once through the barrier I waited with the others in a covered area, until we were once more reassembled as a group.

I have given the Peruvians some praise for their organisational skills to date, so I think it only fair to now have a little moan about the tickets. There must have been more than one person at fault, because the tickets must have passed through a number of hands. I am now a little surprised that I hadn't been given a three-legged donkey or travelled with a useless masseuse…oh wait that last one did happen. Not being allowed on the bus would have been bad enough, but suppose I had walked up, only to find I wasn't allowed into the sanctuary because of the second issue! In the absence of a ticket booth I would have been at a loss for what to do next.

Oblivious to the entrance-ticket error, I excitedly followed Whilder into the sanctuary, only to frustratingly stop some fifty metres or so later. Here he began the first of several short talks about the site and all I could do was dutifully listen on in silence. While I waited I gave some thought to my clothing – not for the first time on this trip I felt I had made a bad choice. The guides, for their part, had kept on and on about the changeable weather, doomsayers to a man they were. I usually lean towards warmth anyway, if I have a choice to make, as I reason I can always take something off if I get too hot. But in the sanctuary, there was very little in the way of shade and it was starting to get warm even at this early hour. I had partially rectified the situation at the entrance by stowing my raincoat away in my daypack, but that still left me wearing a jumper over a long-sleeved thermal top.

While I of course continued to pay attention to Whilder's knowledgeable utterances, my real focus was naturally on the sights all around me. To my left there was a large stepped grassy bank rising upwards, part of a large man-made terrace, which continued on down to my right. Directly in front, all I could see were the end elevations of three stone buildings. The original thatched roofs had long since disappeared, but replacements were fitted to two of the structures to serve as examples of how they used to look. Presumably they used very similar materials, tools and construction methods during this restoration process.

When Whilder had finished speaking we continued forward and down, with each step revealing a little more of the site. As we passed the three buildings, which were now high above us and to our left, we entered a pathway containing wooden barriers. Adaptations to this part of the walkway had to be made as this wasn't the original entrance used by the Incas.

The sanctuary was actually larger than I had imagined or interpreted from photos on the internet. It is reportedly spread across three hundred square kilometres, although not all the space is taken up by buildings or other pieces of stonework.

I soon began to see more and more terraces, which on this occasion were built to help preserve the integrity of the mountainside rather than for growing crops. As we advanced further I discovered that in order to navigate ourselves around we had to climb up and down multitudes of steps. Although my hiking on this trip had been somewhat limited I was starting to find the tour a little tiring.

We stopped outside the Main Temple, a three-sided, roofless structure that had been badly affected by subsidence in its foundations. When facing the back wall, it was noticeable that the right-hand side had dropped several centimetres, loosening the stones. It also looked as if it had been built in two stages as the foundations were made of huge, neatly hewn stones, each weighing several metric tonnes. The upper parts were smaller but still almost a metre in length.

Although it continued to be a little frustrating having to keep stopping to listen to Whilder talk, the information he provided was at times both interesting and invaluable. Without his intervention I would have walked passed the Inti Watana (hitching post of the sun) stone, believing it to be an oddity in terms of design, but certainly not a timepiece. It was just a shame that there were no benches provided as we could have taken the opportunity to use these stops to have a brief rest; as it was, we had to remain standing while listening.

We soon entered an area with the highest concentration of buildings – probably the living quarters, given their size and proximity to each other. This was the most photographed and recognisable section of the whole site. The roofs were all missing which allowed for optional views inside from afar, rather than having to venture down the steps to view up-close. The stonework was, in the main, all of a manageable size, undoubtedly making the transportation and handling of the raw materials less of a chore for the builders. Upon closer inspection, these walls were double-lined and had earth in the cavities for insulation or stability purposes. This is similar to the way we build houses today, with the cavity either left open to allow the air to circulate or filled with insulation.

Most of these buildings had windows which were rather narrow and would not have let in much light. I could also see several small alcoves had been built into the walls to accommodate ornaments or other items. Maybe these had once held the relics I saw in the Museo Larco or maybe some candles to provide extra light. We followed the twisting and turning path through the maze of ancient claustrophobic buildings, feeling the cold stone walls with our hands as we passed through. When we emerged on the other side, the stone flooring was replaced by the much-trodden earthen paths once more.

I had up until now found it very difficult to take in the entire site from just one position, but we soon reached some high ground where the view became clearer. For me the most remarkable point about this site was the quantity of granite stones required to build it; there were tens of thousands on view. It must have been a monumental undertaking to deliver this quantity of raw materials to the stonemasons. They in turn had their work cut out shaping them, ready to be used in the erection of the buildings. The tools they used were extremely rudimentary in the absence of iron, so they must have struggled with the alternatives.

I have been critical of the location of some the Inca sites, as I am a practical person by nature. But here, I have to say looking out over the mountains, the views were stunning. I think if I had lived in those times (and had the authority) I too may have ordered a city to be built up here. Only I would have given them some additional instructions...call me when you are finished building it and carry me up there!

After a couple more short stops, it was soon time to head to the entrance of the Huayna Picchu Mountain and begin our climb. In anticipation I now removed and tied my jumper around my waist and rolled up the sleeves of my undershirt. I would later discover I got a little sunburnt on my arms as I neglected to add any sunscreen, which was something I should have anticipated. Up until now I had not given this morning's climb a lot of thought, as there had been so much else to take in.

Only four hundred people per day were allowed to pre-purchase tickets for this mountain. We arrived for the second of the two time slots, between 10:00 and 11:00; the first being between 07:00 and 08:00. Most of the early birds must have been staying at the nearby hotel, unless they did catch the early bus and head straight for this mountain. Before being allowed to enter we first had to sign a register, noting our names, ages, gender and nationalities. Presumably this was so we could be counted in and out.

I knew the climb was going to be tough, so I selected the slower members of the group to follow; I had a fair idea who they were, judging by yesterday's hike. I wasn't looking to impress anyone by bounding along at the front. Frank and, in particular, his wife Olga seemed to struggle the most, as he didn't like heights and she was not as fit as the others. I would say this was certainly the most physically challenging climb I have ever encountered; in essence it was just one long winding staircase.

Stone steps had helpfully been installed and although they were not exactly uniform, they did make the going a lot easier than the earlier jungle trek. There were even spaces made to allow people to either overtake or pass in the opposite direction. Step by step I climbed, placing one foot in front of the other with only the promise of the summit to welcome me.

Halfway up and the overall layout of Machu Picchu was revealed, but rather frustratingly the higher I climbed, the further away I got, laterally. This made the photographs less detailed and more focussed on the outline. From this distance the city's topography was revealed in a way that couldn't be seen up-close, amid the ruins themselves. I had thought that the city was constructed in between the Huayna Picchu and Machu Picchu Mountains. But from this viewpoint it was clear to see that it was firmly sited on the mountain it was named after. To the left, the twisting, turning road we had travelled up by bus was also clearly visible from here.

At the three-quarter mark we reached a point of no return – a signpost advised us it was now to be one-way only. The path had narrowed quite significantly to allow passage up and around the top of the mountain before rejoining the trail back down at this point. I had initially intended to only go halfway up, as I was really only after a photo opportunity of Machu Picchu and not overly concerned about this challenge. But that was until I was actually on the mountain; now I was of the opinion it was there, it had to be conquered.

We soon reached a structure which served as a resting point, which made a nice change. As with the buildings below, the gabled roof was missing its thatched covering. The stones were small, ranging from palm size to twice that amount. In terms of quantity there must have been thousands, as the walls were two stones wide and very solid looking. There was some kind of mortar in between, making it look like it had been restored by latter-day peoples. There were also narrow windows in the side looking down on the valley below. In a castle they would have been slanting down and used to fire arrows at marauding invaders; here they were perpendicular to the structure and less sinister looking.

It took a while for Olga to join us as she was slow and had also stopped off to find a happy rock, but we were all pleased when her head finally appeared over the wall; we had made it this far as a team after all. I decided, after a short rest, to move on and get a little ahead of the group. Rather than constantly lagging behind, I would take a slow and steady walk to the top, which couldn't be far away. I had paced myself quite well so far and if the others wished to overtake me, I would accommodate them, if the path allowed. At the far side of the structure I found a doorway, and when I looked out and to the right I found more steps leading upward.

Once at the top (2,667m) the view was amazing, but really not too dissimilar to halfway up where I took the photos of Machu Picchu. Despite this observation I was still glad I had chosen to continue to the top as another challenge had been faced and decisively completed. After another short rest, we took a brief look around before heading back down a different path.

I found the downward route a lot easier to navigate and I scrambled along quite easily, leading the way with Amy. There was one part which was a tight squeeze and it looked more like the entrance to a cave than a descending path. The floor was also at an angle so I had to slide downward and off to the right for a few metres; this really was a leap of faith. Emerging from the semi-darkness I thankfully found myself on a platform and not flying through the air. This could have easily been one last trick played by the Incas, making us all human sacrifices. Here I found people attending group-photo sessions with Machu Picchu, of course, in the background. Once we were all reassembled our group took the opportunity to pose as well; this took a while as there were several cameras between us.

As I continued my descent I saw the anxiety in the faces of the people walking up and I was so glad to be heading down. A number of polite exchanges were made, both congratulatory and encouraging in equal measure. I was the second in our group to reach the bottom, with Amy inevitably just ahead. This climb had dominated our morning and now thankfully it was over. I was quite pleased with the speed of my descent, because it meant I now had longer to rest. That is the trouble with being a straggler – by the time you catch up with the group it's time to move on again.

Once we were all assembled at the bottom it was time to say goodbye to those who declined the option of a second day. It was now 12:00, so Melanie, Frank and Olga were informed that they only had an hour left to have a look around. I would have found this extremely disappointing as there was still so much to see. In fact I think I would have decided to give the Huayna Picchu climb a miss, despite the great views it provided, in favour of more exploring. Whilder was heading back immediately and he advised them not to delay their return too long. The bus queues would soon begin to lengthen and they had a train to catch in a few hours. At this news, all three decided not to prolong their stay any longer and immediately headed back with him.

I just had time to thank Melanie for her horse-riding tips over the last five days. It had been good to travel with an experienced horse rider, but one who was just as unfamiliar with the route. I had seen pictures in the brochure of quite large numbers of riders, but for me I was pleased to be travelling with just our small group. I had found the pace set by Oscar and Leo absolutely perfect. Large groups are harder to keep moving; there is always one person who wants to take that last photo or has a problem of some sort, causing a delay.

After our short rest, all the remaining members of the group decided to take a slow walk back towards the main entrance to have lunch. On the way I continued to view the buildings, as well as take lots of photos to add to my swelling collection. Due to the volume of people and narrow paths, our progress was very slow; the day trippers must have just arrived from the train station.

It wasn't hard for me to imagine the site having an unrestricted amount of people, as I have experienced something similar while walking along a section of the Great Wall of China. There were times when I couldn't even see the ground I was walking on, it was so crowded. The section at Badaling is advertised as the most popular part, but only because it is the nearest (renovated) section to Beijing. It is therefore popular with the guides, because it takes less time and effort for them to transport their customers back and forth from their hotels.

Once our bags were retrieved we found the sandwiches, fruit and the fruit juice most welcome after our very active morning. The alternative would have been to use the cafe adjacent to the hotel, but it looked really busy. After our lunch stop, instead of returning to the sanctuary, I decided to head back down to the hotel after all. I was tired, and I reasoned that if I relaxed for the rest of today, I could return tomorrow fully refreshed and raring to go. Yesterday's jungle hike and today's mountain climb had taken more out of me than I cared to admit. If I only had the one day at the site I would have definitely remained and struggled on. The others had decided to do the complete opposite; they would finish viewing the site today, so they had no need to return tomorrow; I could see the merits in both schemes.

On the bus I gave some thought to this morning's visit. Today may have begun with unnecessary confusion over my bus ticket, but, taken as a whole, I had to now consider the trip a success. Admittedly there were still areas within the sanctuary to explore, but that was to be rectified tomorrow when I would venture to the far ends of the site. Although my bus ticket hadn't been an issue on the return journey down the mountain, I would probably have trouble in the morning, but that was for another day. I will save the rest of my thoughts about this wonder of the world until after I have completed both visits.

I spent the afternoon relaxing at the hotel, resting my weary body. An hour before dinner I went for a walk and found the locals engaging in a street parade; there were hundreds filling the streets. The adults were dressed in Peruvian ponchos and hats while the children also wore colourful costumes of their own. The children featured heavily carrying lanterns which lit up the darkness and they also waved paper animals on sticks. They were all heading towards the square I had visited last night; I watched them snake their way up the narrow street without following.

At 19:00, feeling somewhat refreshed I joined Alberto and Marcy, Erwin and Amy for dinner; Lewis and Jyl failed to appear. There was a mix-up when we arrived at the restaurant as we had assumed we were dining in the same section as last night. After a brief discussion we were escorted to another area. Before we were seated we were left to push two tables together to accommodate the number in our group. Because of the confusion I quite wrongly took it upon myself to take a walk to the bar area to look for Lewis and Jyl. I was only trying to be helpful, but I shouldn't have done that; they may have wished to spend some time alone away from the group. My appearance, as well intended as it had been, may have made things awkward for them. As it turned out they were nowhere to be found.

I chose to start with soup (old habits die hard), followed by red trout accompanied by a thick pea puree which tasted a lot better than it looked. I skipped dessert again, but some of them looked good. I shared some red wine with Amy and Erwin; they declined my offer of a second bottle. Just before the end of the meal Lewis and Jyl arrived with some reason for being late, but they didn't drink much either. After dinner I didn't venture outside the complex again as there was little that appealed.

I had hoped tomorrow would go a bit smoother than today as I prefer my adventures that way, but of course that wasn't going to happen. I was to have a most interesting conversation regarding my bus ticket and this time there was no guide to assist me.

CHAPTER THIRTEEN

The Incas

I thought, as I was in between my Machu Picchu visits, that this would be the ideal opportunity to take a break from the trip description and introduce the Inca people. After all, without these individuals I may not have travelled to Peru in the first place and you may well have been reading about a different adventure entirely. In order to ensure my comments are backed up by facts, I have accessed various internet sites; the sources are all listed at the back of the book.

Prior to my trip I viewed the Incas as essentially the equivalent to the North American Indians, in terms of being a primitive culture from a neighbouring part of the world. But while their counterparts in the north mostly lived in wooden, straw or fabric homes, seemingly hardly evolving at all over the years, the Incas went to great pains to build permanent houses of stone. They also learned to innovate and adapt to their harsher environment. Those that lived in the lands to the west of the Andes Mountains in particular had to survive in desert-like conditions, where droughts were common. It was therefore essential that they not only provided themselves with enough water and food for their daily requirements, but also for the leaner times.

To ensure they had a constant supply of water they cut stone channels (aqueducts) into the mountain to transport the life-giving liquid to the heart of their communities, where it was needed most. [3] There it could be used for either drinking, watering crops or bathing. On some occasions they even had a surplus, as the mountains seasonally gave up the melting ice on their peaks. That must have been a nice problem to have – to first of all have nothing and then find your system providing too much. On these occasions they stored the excess in large stone-lined pits. To fix the leaks, in the aqueducts and the pits, they sealed up the holes using clay.

Crops were grown in terraces on the mountains ensuring they used the majority of the land at their disposal. [4] The design and construction of these terraces was the Incas at their creative best. Rather than cut channels into the mountain, they first built stone retaining walls, before adding gravel and sand to the bottom of the newly formed enclosures. This ensured there was adequate drainage, as plants can drown the same as humans with too much water. They then filled the remaining space at the top with a good quality soil, before planting crops such as potatoes and corn. Once the crops were ready for harvesting, they were either consumed immediately or processed and stowed away in stores. With the terraces created to house the nutrient rich soil and the aqueducts providing water, they then entrusted their sun god to take care of the rest.

With the basics of food and water now in plentiful supply, they then turned their attention to other elements of their diet such as protein and calcium. [5] In the absence of cows, pigs and sheep, they ate guinea pig. The rodent was capable of reproducing every three months, thus providing a plentiful supply. Larger animals such as alpacas and llamas not only provided milk, but also raw materials such as fur, used for clothing. When old and no longer of use, the animal was slaughtered for meat and leather. As the empire stretched the length of the western coast of South America, they also added many regional foods to their diet, such as dried fish and chillies.

Despite these innovations, the Incas' way of life may still be perceived as a little primitive by today's standards, and there are a number of reasons for supporting this conclusion. It is said that they never invented the wheel for transport purposes, [6] although there were wheels used on looms and other similar devices. This is understandable in the mountainous parts, but I find it hard to believe that the Incas solely lived on uneven and elevated ground. At its peak the empire totalled ten million people, which would have required a lot of land; there must have been vast areas in between the mountains that were flat. Pack animals such as the alpaca and llamas were used in the absence of horses to carry some supplies, but it must have been a chore for the people having to walk long distances.

Another perceived slight on their character was the failure to invent and use currency. They instead developed a community work-sharing programme, [7] which sounds to me like a form of communism. Everyone in the community was required to make a productive contribution, before sharing in the rewards. There were houses and roads to build, pots and clothing to make, crops to grow and harvest. The government controlled the food production centrally and any excess items (or indeed any other resources) were distributed throughout the realm. Refusal to work or a perceived laziness was punishable by death as the greater good was at stake. A little harsh, but this system provided everyone in the community with the majority of their needs, even healthcare and education. If anything else was needed, they used the barter system when engaging with the neighbouring villages.

In some ways it is a shame we don't use a similar system across the world today. Our brightest and best are developing cures for terrible diseases and conditions, but these medicines and procedures are only sold at a premium to those who can afford it. Richer western communities also have work-shy individuals who expect the central government to provide handouts, without them ever having made a contribution to the society they live in. Then there are couples who produce enormous families and then demand the government house and feed their brood; I find it astonishing that these people are still being so heavily subsidised. While I agree it is their right to reproduce as many times as they want, they shouldn't be paid for doing so – the world is not short of people. If you cannot support twelve children by working for a living, then don't have so many.

The third significant reason for believing the Incas were primitive was the lack of a written language to back up their Quechan tongue. It was a shame they didn't write things down, as we would know a lot more about them today if they did. What we do know of their history was written by the Spanish conquistadores who wrote down stories told to them by their captives.

The Incas did have people who they entrusted with remembering their history, and when this walking-library approach needed supplementing they used a 'knotted' string system called quipu. [8] Although simple in design, it was still essentially a code, which even today is indecipherable as so few examples remain. The system comprised a horizontal bar with various lengths of vertical strings attached. Each dangling string contained a series of knots, each with a different meaning. The type, number and colour of the knots formed the message. This was particularly helpful with figures, but I would imagine the historical facts would have been harder to record and afterwards translate. Although the Spanish were documenting their history, it was born out of a desire to understand the people they were controlling and not for posterity. It is said the conquistadores even destroyed the strings they found, as they were suspicious about their content.

Like all primitive people, it was inevitable they turned to religion and ceremony when things went wrong. [9] If crops failed, it was obvious they had upset their sun god in some way; after all, he usually brought the heat and light they needed on a daily basis. When offerings of food and clothing, etc. proved insufficient to bring about a change in their fortunes, they resorted to more extreme methods such as human sacrifice. Of course, this was not unique to the Incas; it has been prevalent all over the world at one time or another. But what I find irritating is that there always seems to be a weak reason behind the practice. On this occasion it is understood that the Incas tried their best to understand the complexities of nature. They were struggling to comprehend why they were being subjected to natural disasters, such as earthquakes and floods. By drugging and then sacrificing their young children, or captured enemies, they hoped to fend off the bad spirits responsible. It was apparently considered quite an honour to be chosen, as the 'victim' was to ascend to Hanan Pacha (heaven). I wonder from whose perspective this bestowed honour was considered special; did the recipients truly believe they were the fortunate ones?

I always struggle to understand the logic of any form of sacrifice as there must have been a time when the practice clearly wasn't working. Coincidence would account for some of their successes, but there must have also been a very long string of failures. They must have reached a point when they questioned themselves, the process, or the shamans conducting the ceremonies. I was now beginning to form the opinion that the Incas were indeed a very primitive people, in terms of their beliefs and practices at least.

Despite the lack of transport, coinage and written text, the Incas still managed to produce a fairly cultured society (if you ignore the human sacrifice part). They were strong in diplomacy and negotiation, which they used when expanding their empire along the coast. This must have come naturally, an extension of the bartering and labour-use philosophies they employed every day. Initially they camped in large numbers on the outskirts of a village and offered the people the opportunity to keep some part of their society, like their religion, for example. They almost bribed them to join by offering central benefits of food, water, clothing, education, etc. This would have been a big draw to lesser-prepared peoples. However, if this form of negotiation failed, they also had the numbers to be merciless in response and would take what they wanted by force.

After nearly a hundred years expanding their empire, Sapa (King) Huayna Capac was informed that foreigners were exploring within his lands to the north. [10] Although he sought out the Spanish intruders, he failed to find any sign of them; instead he contracted the smallpox virus they had inadvertently brought with them. With no immunity or medicine to treat the condition, he died shortly upon his return. His two sons, Huáscar and Atahualpa, fought over the right of succession in a civil war that was to last for three years. Atahualpa emerged as the victor, but his reign was then cut short by the arrival of the Spanish conquistadores.

There is much written about how a group of soldiers numbering in their hundreds managed to conquer a nation of millions. Face to face, one army to another, this would of course have been settled very quickly in favour of the Incas, so there must have been more to the story than that. I shall now attempt to summarise the key points which brought about the demise of the Inca Empire.

The new Sapa agreed to meet the Spanish leader, Francisco Pizarro, in the town of Cajamarca for talks. [11] He greatly underestimated his opponents due to their small numbers while also being ignorant of their tactics, armament and greed. Leaving most of his vast army on the outskirts of the town, he advanced with only two thousand mostly unarmed men, still a sizable number in comparison to the Spaniards. He believed this show of strength of numbers alone would be enough to scare off the one hundred and eighty soldiers that awaited him. This group would have included all of his chief negotiators, foolishly leaving the bulk of his army without a 'brain', should he fail. Cut off the head of an animal and it will die, no matter how big it is.

Having arrived several hours earlier, Pizarro orchestrated a fierce ambush with riflemen, snipers and finally cavalry charges, slaughtering the vast majority and capturing the rest, including Atahualpa. Pizarro's tactics, superior weapons and armour were all too much for his primitive opponents, despite the ten to one ratio in their favour. The bulk of the remaining army, now leaderless and bewildered at the sudden loss of their betters, simply scattered.

Of course, this wasn't the end of hostilities; they did regroup, but this simple victory was the beginning of the end. In addition to superior tactics and arms, the invaders' numbers were later swelled by Spanish reinforcements and, just as importantly, local tribes who looked to gain from the battles and disruption. The indigenous newcomers realised a little too late who the real enemy were; the conquistadores were never going to share their new-found wealth with strangers.

Atahualpa was later executed when he outlived his usefulness, and his wife was taken by Pizarro. Once the Spanish had seized Cusco and the Sacred Valley area, it was only a matter of time before overall victory was assured. After fighting a civil war and enduring a smallpox epidemic, the Incas were in disarray. Over the next twelve years there were many battles, which were won by using a wide range of strange and foreign weapons. [12] The Inca population had never faced steel swords, steel armour and horsemen using lances. They would not have known about crossbows, single-shot rifles and cannon shot from ships. Using only sling-shot and wooden clubs, their vast numbers were eventually defeated.

Francisco Pizarro was a seasoned campaigner who was lucky to have four brothers available to use as his generals. [13] These trusted allies ensured there were fewer disputes over the vast wealth they accumulated. The supply of gold, silver and precious stones were seemingly beyond measure. To manage such a vast area, the invaders employed similar diplomacy as the Incas, but were far more brutal in their reprisals. When it suited them, they employed the Inca tactic of allowing the regional leaders to stay in place and religious practices to continue, although they immediately imposed Catholicism which was eventually to take hold.

In 1541, nine years into the conquest, Pizarro himself was assassinated by his own people, aged in his sixties. [13] His body was dismembered and his head placed in a box bearing an inscription of his name, which was only discovered in a forgotten crypt in the 1970s. He had taken control by force and then been deposed himself, very much in keeping with the times.

After many years of fighting, the Spanish foothold was irretrievably embedded in Peru and South America in general. The Incas paid a heavy price for not developing their weapons and wartime tactics. Gold, silver and many other gems were spirited away to Spain helping to fund future expeditions in other lands. But it wasn't only jewels that the Incas lost to the invaders; their bloodline has now been mixed with the Spanish. Today there are still some that speak the Quechan language and there are some ceremonies that are kept alive, but the Incas in their purest form are no more.

CHAPTER FOURTEEN

Machu Picchu revisited

Next morning, I awoke typically early and feeling reasonably refreshed after a really good night's sleep. I ventured down for breakfast at 06:00 to find I was not alone in the restaurant, although there was no one from the group present. I had given serious thought to catching an early bus, but, given that I had already visited the sanctuary and was not under any real time pressures, I decided against it. Altogether I would probably have six hours or so to explore the remainder of the site and that should prove sufficient.

As I left the restaurant and headed back to my room I met Marcy on her way to breakfast. The others would definitely not be returning to Machu Picchu today; the next time we would meet up would be at the train station for the return to Cusco. This now felt like one of my usual trips where I am a lone traveller, free to take my time and organise myself anyway I chose. I suppose the only thing missing is the company, the feeling of sharing a moment, a common experience, with another person.

Before I set off to join the bus queue I had some packing to do. It took a while to squeeze all my belongings back into the blue duffel bag, making me wonder how I had managed the first time round. I wasn't overly concerned about the heavily creased clothing as I had other items back in Cusco and even a reliable laundry service if required. Once packed, I attached a new label, and dropped the bag off at the reception desk ready for collection by the porters. I also checked out of the hotel as I had no intention of returning by 12:00. I still took my daypack, but I packed very light with just the essentials: a couple of bottles of water, suntan lotion, mosquito spray, that sort of thing.

Before joining the bus queue, I of course had to pay a visit to the ticket booth, which was not something I was looking forward to. Yesterday, Whilder had told me he would speak to the vendor and a replacement ticket would be forthcoming, but I remained unconvinced. Rather worryingly I didn't have S/.80 in cash on me if I had to purchase a new one, as I had given the last of my Peruvian currency to Claudio for his tip. Hopefully my bankcard would suffice and, presumably, buying a new ticket was an option, otherwise why else would they have a ticket booth?

I approached the window and presented my original ticket and identification, before giving a brief explanation about the issue, noting that I had the salesperson's full attention. She listened with the intensity of someone either struggling with the language, my accent or the situation as it was being explained. When I had finished speaking it was obvious that she had no idea what I was talking about. Whilder hadn't spoken to her and I would not be receiving a replacement ticket. Not yet ready to admit defeat, I politely, but firmly, continued the discussion. When I had exhausted all possible arguments and just about given up hope, she made one last surprising statement. It seemed I would not be receiving a new ticket because the one in my possession was valid for three days!

I left the booth at 07:20 too relieved to be angry at the incompetent fools who had put me through this stressful time and joined the now very long queue for the bus. As I neared the front I spotted my friend from yesterday who was once again diligently booking people on board. My heart sank a little at this discovery as I had hoped it would be someone else, someone who knew the rules regarding the ticket validity. As I inched along I asked several people to check my ticket. These individuals included tour guides and I even plucked up the courage to ask someone in uniform as he was passing.

All agreed I had no issue, despite the date.

Even though I now knew I was in the right, I also knew I wouldn't win any argument. Yesterday Whilder had a real battle on his hands debating some sort of point and he spoke the language. If I was refused entry to the bus again I would have to return to the ticket booth and insist on buying another ticket; I would then have to join the queue again which would be extremely annoying. My only other option would be to forget the bus and try to hike up the mountain. Yesterday I had noticed there were small staircases bisecting the twisting roads. The problem with this option was the effort and time it would require. When I finally reached the sanctuary I would be exhausted and in no mood to then go exploring with the short time I had left. Walking was truly the last resort and one I really didn't want to undertake.

At the door to the bus I nervously presented my ticket to the inspector, while deliberately keeping my thumb over the printed date. As before the bar code was scanned by her handheld device, only this time I was waved straight on board. There was none of the fuss from yesterday; my thumb had taken the human element out of the equation and allowed the technology to do its job. I had thought that the journey over the Andes would be the difficult part of this trip, not acquiring a bus ticket for the last leg up the mountain. I did face a similar check on the way down, but yesterday those people seemed less rigorous in their approach.

As I write and recall the situation it still doesn't make sense that the ticket was deemed fit to use. That three-day scenario should be for the date of travel and the two days that followed, not the day before the date on the ticket. The lesson here is to always check your paperwork and take nothing for granted; I could have resolved this situation when we were first given the tickets. Whilder could then have visited the ticket booth early the first morning and been better informed about our situation.

At 08:25 I passed through the turnstiles and entered the sanctuary once more, but instead of rushing ahead I stopped to read the plaques on the wall, which were on the left, just past the sheltered entrance. The first commemorated the site's construction from 1450-1540 commending the builders for their design and build achievement. The text was in Spanish, but had several words like civil, avances, ingenieria, construccion that were discernible to an Englishman. The next plaque celebrated seventy-five years since the discovery of the site (1911-1986) and was donated by the Peruvian tourist board. A third plaque, dated 1911-2011, was bestowed by the Cusco rotary club to celebrate a hundred years since the scientific discovery of the site.

Lastly, there was a plaque dedicated to Hiram Bingham from the people of Cusco thanking him for the (re)discovery of Machu Picchu. Fitted in 1948, it seemingly took thirty-seven years to acknowledge the service this man had given to their country. Perhaps he was remembered due to the release of his book in the same year. The book described in fine detail how he led a team to discover the ruins of the city. It was, however, full of embellishments as the story had been regaled so many times over the years, changing a little in each telling. For example, in the book he knew the significance of his finding immediately, while in reality it was only upon his return with reinforcements that the enormity of the site was revealed. The small size of the plaque, in comparison to the others, gives the impression that the patrons were still annoyed at him for stealing the tens of thousands of artefacts that belonged to their ancestors. He reportedly operated a 'finders keepers' policy when the Peruvian government wanted them back after his analysis.

I was dressed more appropriately today, probably for the first time on this trip. I wore a tee-shirt with a light zipped jumper, loose trousers and trainers. There was some heat from the early morning sun, but that was offset by a cool breeze which was most welcome. Most people I came across just wore tee-shirts, but I was happier with these layers. Once again it felt nice not having anyone telling me what to do or how long to spend looking at any of the structures. I was finally at my target destination and in control of my own destiny, at least for a few hours anyway. At the back of my mind was the meeting time for the train and my departure back to Cusco.

After taking several more photos and having fellow tourists assist with taking others of me (with my camera, not theirs – that would have been weird), it was time for today's main challenge. Yesterday I had spotted a sign directing people up some steps to the Sun Gate (Inti Punku). When I say some steps, I may be understating it somewhat; it looked like it would take hours to complete the return trip. The others hiked the path yesterday which, combined with days of trekking and the Huayna Picchu climb, was quite an impressive feat. I think if I had attempted it, I would have spent the whole of today in bed, given how I felt yesterday. I had been pre-warned that there would be a certain amount of physical activity, but I still had some days left of my trip, so I needed to pace myself sufficiently.

I set off on the trail with the main site and Huayna Picchu behind and over my left shoulder. The one-and-a-half-metre-wide path had a slight incline to begin with and was also extremely uneven. Stones had been laid to form a pathway, but they either weren't fitted correctly in the first place or had been dislodged over time, probably the latter. I initially had to select which individual stone to place my foot on with each step I took, which made for hard going. In fact, this section of the path would have been a lot better without the stones. I think if I had been restoring the site the paths would have been one of the first things I would have attended to. If the people could move around a little quicker they could view the site and depart faster, allowing more people to be ushered in.

There was a two metre-high stone wall to my right, holding back the mountain, and downward to my left there were several small terraces sloping away. I looked into the distance, but it was unclear where my final destination lay as the dark green foliage masked the view. In fact it was hard to see any pathway along the route, beyond the stone trail directly ahead of me. This was not too dissimilar to some of the trails I rode with Caesar.

Once this initial phase was navigated I found the next section far more agreeable. I was also provided some welcome shade, formed by an avenue of overhead trees and it was here I stopped occasionally for my short rest breaks. I was determined to take my time this morning and enjoy my walk. It was nice to stop whenever I liked; as well as resting up I could take photos and greet the passing fellow travellers.

As I progressed the elevation increased slightly, and I began to encounter walls constructed with a little more refinement. Rather than mere piles of stones selected for their size and shape, these had clearly been cut to fit snugly together. This was more in keeping with my perception of Inca building techniques. I thought at this stage I must be nearing the Sun Gate and the end of my expedition, but I was in fact only half-way to my goal. My unfamiliarity with the route was the only problem I had today, which made it difficult to pace myself.

The view from this vantage point was now similar to the one I enjoyed on yesterday's climb. Although Huayna Picchu appeared quite large to those who stood up close intending to climb it, it was in fact dwarfed by the surrounding peaks, a mere pimple on the landscape. I was sure if I pointed it out to passers-by and declared I had scaled it the day before, they wouldn't have been overly impressed. This mini-hike was really putting things into perspective; it seems there is always one more mountain to climb.

I soon passed a small group of roofless, open-fronted buildings where a workman was carrying out repairs. He was stooped atop a three-metre section of wall, diligently toiling in the hot sun. He was sporting a white builder's hardhat which surprised me somewhat as without a chinstrap it would be of little use. There was nothing above to fall on him and if he fell from his current position, the protective hat would have been dislodged before he hit the ground. Maybe he was using it to keep the sun off his head?

Steps and even handrails were now starting to appear as I trudged ever nearer to my destination. After a few more bends I spotted the beginning of more terraces and there were groups of people congregating above me. I knew then I was very close to the end. After one hour and forty minutes I finally reached the Sun Gate. A sign indicated I was now at an elevation of 2,720m so I calculated I had ascended nearly three hundred metres vertically. I could have completed the hike in half the time I did, as I had only travelled two kilometres, but most of the terrain had prevented me from rushing to the summit even if I had the inclination to try.

The Sun Gate was made up of roofless rooms, all set at slightly different elevations due to the landscape. It was originally the main entrance to the site, where soldiers stood on guard. The most distinctive parts, and what made them unmistakably of Inca design to me, were the head-height trapezoid insets within. They were narrower at the top than the bottom and looked like windows with the outer side bricked up. As with the collection of rooms far below, these were probably used to hold candles or objects. One of the tourists had wedged their blue rucksack in one of them…now that just seemed wrong.

These structures would have originally housed soldiers as it was once the main entrance to the site. This location was chosen as the summer solstice sun shone through the structure, which was very important from a spiritual perspective. The Incas worshipped many deities, but they believed their rulers were descendants of the sun god, Inti. Although a primitive outlook in some ways, I can at least understand why they revered the sun. It provided heat and light, which helped crops to grow, illuminated their narrow stone paths (particularly this one) and brought a sense of well-being to the community. They had little else to worry about until the Spanish arrived.

After spending another ten minutes viewing the ruins I decided it was time to make my way back down. As I now had a fair idea of the distance, I stopped less frequently and completed the descent in just one hour. At the end of the trail I was back amongst the buildings of the main site with a decision to make. I just about had the strength for one more trek, but did I have the time? It was now 11:15 and I was stood before a sign directing people up to the Inca Bridge. As I gave consideration to the time I had left, I slowly started up the steep staircase towards it. It made no sense to be stationary while I contemplated my options, as there would be places to explore on the way even if I didn't commit to reaching it.

I knew I had about four hours left, before the train departed, but I couldn't afford to miss it as transport for the last leg to Cusco had been arranged at the other end. As well as allowing reasonable times for the remaining tasks I also had to allow some contingency as things could go wrong. If this next walk of discovery turned out to be as long as the Sun Gate trek I would struggle to return back down much before 13:30. I then needed time for queuing for the bus, at peak time; Whilder had yesterday warned the departing group about this problem. I might have issues with my bus ticket and when I made it down I still had the walk to the train station where I then had to locate my luggage. I had all of these tasks ahead of me with only a rough idea how long each one would take to complete, and I also had to allow some time for lunch.

As I strode purposefully upward I looked to the mountain up ahead and it did seem a little daunting; it was a lot steeper than my last expedition and I really had no idea how far it was to the bridge. I now regretted not carrying out more research prior to travelling, but I hadn't expected the site to be spread out in this fashion and I certainly hadn't expected distances to be an unknown quantity. Most of the photos indicated the site was just the collection of buildings in front of Huayna Picchu. I was also allocated a guide for the first day, so I reasoned he would answer any questions I had. The problem with this assumption was that he had departed before I knew that these places existed.

After much deliberation I decided to err on the side of caution and abandon the Inca Bridge hike. I would have liked to have seen it, but only so I could satisfy myself that I had walked and viewed all the site had to offer. The bridge was previously an alternative back entrance into the site and just a very narrow path adjacent to the mountain wall. The Sun Gate by comparison had been no different to the rest of the main site in terms of structure design, but as it was the original main entrance, I was glad that I took the time to visit it.

Having completed one flight of the steep steps, I now found myself on a grassy terraced area where llamas were grazing. These native beasts were added for effect and seemed completely oblivious to the hordes of tourists around them. From this elevation the views were not that different to those below, but I spent my remaining time here, viewing the site and taking photos from as many different angles as possible. Without the visit to the Inca Bridge there was now little else I hadn't seen, so after a further fifteen-twenty minutes I headed back down, taking a slow circular route towards the exit.

Passing through the turnstiles, I joined a small queue of people who were rubber-stamping their passports with the Machu Picchu logo, a last souvenir of the visit. I then joined the long queue for the buses and awaited my transport down the mountain. It was just as well the site had now a limited amount of people each day; the previous queues must have been horrendous. A pictorial sign on my left indicated it was 1.748 kilometres walk down to the town which would take approximately one hour to complete.

I was actually on board the bus after only thirty minutes, my trusty thumb working in my favour again. After a further twenty minutes I was back at Aguas Calientes and in familiar surroundings once more. It was now 12:30, a lot earlier than I had expected as everything had gone smoothly. I now had three hours to kill before the train arrived. I spent the first hour having some lunch, the second hour having a massage, and arrived at the train station with an hour to spare. I spent this remaining time searching for my luggage and checking the train details. It didn't take long to find my bag amongst a large pile in an area allocated to the Inkaterra Pueblo hotel. I was a little surprised that nobody challenged me when I removed it and headed for the indoor seating area.

The station was packed with people who had all completed their visits to Machu Picchu. As I waited I turned my thoughts to my visits. First of all, I have to say the sanctuary is deserving of its status of being one of the wonders of the world. The site is huge, the buildings still remain mostly in situ and the location is inspiring to look upon (not to mention a challenge to get to). It was also very clever of the organisers to create the Inca and Salkantay trails, as there was no question that the journey across the mountains plays a huge part in the overall experience. Trips of this nature usually err on the easier side of travel whenever possible; in other countries I suspect the only option would have been the train.

I was glad I had taken up the option of the second day to explore the site, although I don't think I made the best use of either day. On day one I should have taken a long rest after lunch and then completed the long journey to the Sun Gate and got it out of the way. The site closes at 18:00 so I had plenty of time; easy to say as I now sit and write about the experience. I could then have dedicated the second day to climbing up to the Inka Bridge. Pictures make it look an extremely dangerous path, as the trail is no more than a metre wide with the mountain on one side and a sheer drop on the other. They have installed shoulder-height guide ropes, which look to me as if harnesses are supposed to be attached – they are not much use otherwise. Despite the shortcomings of day one I could still have done more the today, but I allowed far too much contingency, without needing any of it. On another day it may have been very different.

Although Leo did everything he was asked, and more besides, he failed to provide us with any tips regarding the site visit itself. I wasn't present for any of the hikers' meetings so I don't know if they were given any guidance by Whilder. He had certainly visited the sanctuary on numerous occasions, so he could have suggested a route or the best way of spending our time. Overall I am very happy with my visits, but in a very small way I have some regrets, as I feel I left it somewhat unfinished.

It took another forty minutes for the others to arrive with their luggage and we passed the remaining time swapping stories about our day. No matter how much or how little I achieved on day one, I was always going to go back for the second day. The rest of the group had spent a leisurely morning in the hotel's grounds, deservedly relaxing after all the hiking they had done over the last few days. They had expected to see me at lunch at the hotel, but I was never going to walk back to the furthest part of the town to eat at a hotel I had checked out of. They had then stopped off for mojitos and actually saw me heading for the train station, but when they called I was too far away to hear them. I had missed out on some alcohol then – now that was a serious revelation.

At 15:30 we boarded the train and departed twenty minutes later. I was separated from the others once more as the seats were allocated by number, but I did have one of the best seats. As with the coach to Cusco I was right at the very front, which provided great views to my left, above and straight ahead. Curiously we had knives and forks set in front of us, which proved to be a little over the top for the single sweet pastry they later served.

After the remnants of the food were cleared we were informed that there would be some entertainment to follow. The nature of the first performance was a little unexpected to say the least. Without warning a character wearing a bright yellow, shoulder-length wig and a red and black devil's mask leapt into the carriage. His costume was completed by a full-length multi-coloured coat, with large red scorpions emblazoned on the front. It was hard to tell if he was a clown or a devil; whichever of the two you decided upon, he was truly the stuff of children's nightmares.

To assist the character with his performance, shrill piccolo music was piped into the carriages via the public address system; the passengers, for their part, started rhythmically clapping along. Seemingly encouraged by their response, he began shaking a short red cane above his head while running up and down the aisle. Thankfully, he didn't quite reach my position. I couldn't work out if he was attempting to ward off bad spirits or he was the bad spirit. Young children would have been terrified, which would have made the exhibition worthwhile (for me) had there been any. Their screams would have added quite nicely to the cacophony of noise and chaos unfolding before us.

Shortly after the devil/clown had departed, a more sedate fashion show began, which allowed everyone's blood pressure to return to normal. Locals paraded in clothing made from alpaca and other native animals. Each item was of course for sale and I thought that quite an enterprising idea, taking advantage of the captive audience in this way. At home all I usually get on trains are Romanians begging for money to feed their constantly sick child. Here the intention was similar – they wanted money, but I felt a lot less inclined to curse the individuals.

The journey to Ollantaytambo train station took one hour and thirty-five minutes to travel the ninety-two kilometres. At the station we were met by our minibus driver who allowed some of the group a few minutes to browse the wares in a local shop, while the rest of us stretched our legs. We finally set off to Cusco at 17:45, which, although another beginning, was to be the final leg of today's long journey. It was getting dark now and we faced another hour and forty minutes on the road. Halfway into the drive I started to feel a little tired and I could also feel the familiar effects of altitude sickness beginning to return.

As we neared the hotel I began to recognise the area, so, knowing I was soon to depart, I gave some thought to my goodbye speech; they were a good group and I wanted to thank them properly. Suddenly, I felt a jolt and heard a muffled cry from Jyl who was behind me and to my left. The driver immediately pulled over to the side of the road and turned off the engine. I didn't know what had happened at this stage, but it sounded and felt like something really heavy had fallen over in the back. We had in fact been heavily sideswiped by another vehicle. Jyl had seen the incident unfold, hence her exclamation, and described to us every detail while our driver checked his vehicle over. Apparently, a car, driven by an East-Asian-looking gentleman, had exited a side turning (from our left-hand side) onto the main road. He would have hit us square-on if he hadn't turned away at the last moment. As it was, the glancing blow left damaged panels half the length of our left-hand side. Given that we were on the right-hand side of the road, the driver had to cross an empty lane before he hit us, making the accident even more bewildering.

The two drivers spoke for an age, even engaging a local passer-by to act as an arbitrator. I couldn't comprehend the length of time it took to sort out the issue. All they had to do was swap insurance details and move on. The alternative would have been for our driver to grab him by the throat and roll around on the floor. Either way, it shouldn't have taken the best part of an hour that it did before we moved on. Even more annoyingly I was only a few minutes' drive away from my hotel; I could have walked if it weren't for my luggage. The unnecessary stop at the shop as we left the train had put us in this location, at exactly this time. When we finally got underway I was indeed deposited outside my hotel only five minutes later, but still an hour later than expected.

After exchanging farewells with my travelling companions, I wearily trudged up the steps to reception. It was 20:30 and I figured I just had enough strength to walk to a local bar, down a few well-deserved beers and have something to eat. It had been a long journey and I now had a mild case of altitude sickness, but at least today's adventure was at an end, or so I thought. In the last few days I had endured a mix-up with my bus ticket and a car crash, now fate was to take one more swipe at me.

After being warmly welcomed back and having my booking confirmed at reception, I was then informed that my room was unavailable. It seemed that the previous occupant had been taken ill so the hotel had extended the persons stay; altitude sickness no doubt. I didn't take the news very well, if I am being honest, as I was tired and not feeling that good myself. I suggested the best place for Goldilocks was in hospital. I mean, in my humble opinion, if the person was so ill that they couldn't be moved to another hotel then they should seek medical attention.

My protestations were a little unexpected, judging by the reactions from the staff, and of course, completely pointless. I got the impression this wasn't the first time this had happened and they considered the situation quite normal. An alternative hotel had already been arranged for me and the taxi to transport me to my new home was on its way. My stored belongings arrived right on cue just as the car pulled up outside and I left them to be loaded on board by the staff. The concierge came with me to pay the taxi and assist with booking me in…all part of the service.

As we drove I began to question the location of the new hotel as we were heading steadily uphill and noticeably away from the main square. I explained to the concierge that the main reason for selecting his hotel in the first place was its close proximity to the bars and restaurants. After five minutes we stopped outside the Hilton Garden Inn, ironically located across the road from the car accident, a mere hundred metres away. My accompanying friend brought my luggage in, but didn't get a tip as he left to return to his hotel; in fact, he was lucky not to get the tip of my boot up his posterior when he left me at the new reception desk.

Once in my room I had a quick shower, took an altitude sickness tablet and departed the hotel. I could have called a taxi, but I was impatient to get to a bar and still a little annoyed at recent developments. I thought a fifteen to twenty minute walk would help to clear my head and improve my mood. Unfortunately, the hotel was at the top of a steep hill and there were hundreds and hundreds of steps to descend. I felt every one of those steps through my aching knees; I didn't know whether to laugh or cry as I trudged slowly down.

On my previous visit I had found Cusco to be a quiet place in terms of nightlife. Maybe there were other livelier places hidden in the backstreets, but all I had found were small restaurants with bars attached almost as an afterthought. I wasn't physically able or mentally up to exploring the surrounding streets at this hour, so I just headed for the nearest restaurant. As I undecidedly browsed a menu outside one establishment I was accosted by an old woman who almost forcibly dragged me to another place across the road. If I had been the owner of the first restaurant, I would have been a little annoyed; for my part, I was too tired to argue.

I ordered a bottle of Cusquena, which of course had a picture of Machu Picchu on the label. This brought my day full circle and as I waited for my pizza I gave further thought to my trip so far. I had actually enjoyed the physical challenge the lodge to lodge trek had provided, even now, despite my aches and pains. Now that part of the trip was over I was almost at a loss as to how to replace that feeling. I did have one last big adventure lined up, but flying over the Nazca Lines would be a different type of experience altogether. For that trip it would be my nerves that would be tested and not my physical prowess.

The pizza wouldn't have won any awards for its presentation, but it was hot and I had no complaints about the taste. Soon after finishing my meal I decided to head back to the hotel and seek out the bar; it couldn't have been quieter than this restaurant. I asked the staff to call me a taxi as I had no intention of tackling another mountain tonight. Instead of making a phone call though, one of the staff surprised me by running out into the street and hailing a passing vehicle; it was probably a taxi.

Back at the Hilton I spent the last few hours of my day sat at the bar chatting to the barman about my trip and in particular my day. Although priced the same as my previous establishment, I found this place a little soulless and cold. It was as if everything was made of stainless-steel (it wasn't') and its target customers were businessmen in grey flannel suits.

I was now completely relaxed and didn't even complain when I had to settle for Tanqueray gin in the absence of my much-preferred Gordon's. As the latter part of the day had ended a little flat, the barman decided to cheer me up with an invitation to join him and his friends at tomorrow's Corpus Christi festival. There would be traditional food, including the much-coveted rodents, and we would have lots to drink. Although I had an afternoon flight to catch, I couldn't think of a better way to end my visit to Cusco, so I accepted. With the meeting time and place agreed, I headed off to bed.

CHAPTER FIFTEEN

Corpus Christi

My first task this morning was to email the Mountain Lodges of Peru to inform them about their blue duffel bag's new location. But unfortunately, due to their Corpus Christi holiday, all I received was an out of office reply, which left me to ponder the method of its return. I hadn't the desire to return to the other hotel, as I felt I hadn't left on particularly good terms. While I considered my options, I transferred my belongings back into my main case and prepared for departure. Checkout was a rather surprisingly early time of 10:00, which I knew would soon come around if I dallied too long. Once packed, I left my camera and laptop on charge and took a shower.

At 09:30, just as I was about to depart my room, reception called to inform me I had a visitor. It seemed Leo had tracked me down after all, so the duffel bag problem was now resolved. He had no doubt been informed of the new arrangements when he arrived at my previous place of residence. I brought my bags down and met him in reception where we shared a warm greeting and a pleasant, but informative, chat about my adventures since we last met. Being a reasonable sort of chap, he agreed that the hotel situation could have been handled better and the other person should have been asked to vacate the room. I had got the incident off my chest last night, chatting to the underemployed barman and had moved on. I prefer not to dwell on these things as they can leave you feeling bitter.

After Leo departed I took a seat in reception and opened my trusty laptop. I had spent some time in my room trying to print off my flight voucher, but without success. I prefer to present some sort of paperwork at the airport, rather than just a quoted reference number or an e-ticket on a smart phone (I haven't embraced that type of technology as yet). Once again the Wi-Fi code was active and the printer was visible to my laptop – all I had to do now was press print and the paperwork would be spirited off to the concierge desk.

Once again it failed, which did not come as a complete surprise to me as I don't have a lot of luck when it comes to computers. Now in reception, I had convinced myself that if I tried again I could now 'will' the pages to appear, but it wasn't to be. After several failed attempts, I turned to the helpful woman behind the desk and asked her to print off a copy via my memory stick. I was half expecting to be lectured about company rules concerning computer viruses, but all was fine.

With my paperwork now in order I deposited my bags in a locked room adjacent to reception and left the hotel in search of some food. I could have dined in the hotel breakfast room, but I was curious to see what the locals had to offer. At the same time I was also conscious of not going too far; it was now 10:30 and I had to walk back up the steep mountain of steps to meet Carlos the barman in an hour. Within a few minutes I found a small place where locals were eating, but as the members of staff were all too busy in the kitchen to even acknowledge me, I left; I don't do waiting of that nature.

Across the road I found El Sabor Norteno, a 'Cebicheria' restaurant, which I later learned meant it was a venue that specialises in the fish dish – ceviche. I took a seat in the back room and perused the faded and creased menu. This type of place was off the beaten track and not as popular as the restaurants on the main square. To my dismay I found myself ordering a cheese burger and a pineapple milkshake instead of something more traditional. This was mainly because they were two of the few things I recognised on the menu that looked even remotely appetising. It was a little too heavy for breakfast, bearing in mind I was soon to eat at the festival, but I thought it best to line my stomach now with comfort food before sampling the local beer.

The dining area was divided into two rooms linked by a narrow opening; in fact, it looked more like someone's home than a restaurant. There was barely enough room to seat more than ten people and the tables were set out in a rather haphazard manner. Rustic, I think would be a good description, but it was clean and the owner friendly. When the food was brought to the table, everything looked fine; the milkshake was served in a tall glass and tasted good, but the burger (although edible) was not entirely to my liking. It didn't taste or look like 100% beef, but then again I suppose it wasn't advertised as such.

I think there were a number of eateries in the area where I could have played the 'guess the meat' game.

After breakfast I left for my rendezvous, which was to be at the bus stop, just around the corner from the hotel. As I sat waiting I had a chance to look around and people watch. A few bus drivers beeped at me as they approached to see if I wanted them to stop. They seemed to operate a hail and ride system rather than a scheduled stopping service. High up in a churchyard across the road a young couple were having a massive argument. He must have made a serious mistake because he was getting a huge telling off. The finger-wagging and nagging went on for at least fifteen minutes; for the most part he hung his head in shame, without offering any sort of explanation. Latin women seem to be very forthcoming with their opinions and don't exactly suffer in silence.

I waited until 11:45, which was fifteen minutes longer than we agreed, but he didn't show up. Maybe his friends weren't struck on the idea of him bringing a tourist along. I decided not to waste any more time and headed back down to join the throngs of people at the festival. In these circumstances it is usually the drunken customer that makes all the promises the night before and fails to show up. I wasn't too bothered, but it had slightly affected my plans this morning. I could have gone straight to the festival and eaten there, before wandering around having a beer or two. Anything would have been better than just hanging around waiting for a no-show.

Cusco has a number of squares, but I had a very good idea which one to head for, as I had passed through it last night on my way to the pizza restaurant. There had been hundreds of stall frames waiting to be set up and a long line of light grey portable toilets were also arranged at the entrance to the square. This wasn't a one-off celebration and so the organisers were well prepared for the thousands of people that would attend.

The Corpus Christi (body of Christ) festival was introduced by the Spanish conquistadores in an attempt to overshadow the Inca Inti Raymi (Festival of the Sun) celebration. Today they celebrate both, within a few weeks of each other, presumably soon after embracing Catholicism as their main religion. Even though I don't share their beliefs, it was nice to learn the Inca descendants hadn't abandoned all of their ancestors' traditions.

In contrast to last night, I now found the square to be packed full of people as well as the now-colourful stalls, most of which were under canopies or large umbrellas to keep the sun off the food and, more importantly, the ice buckets of beer. I headed for the centre of the festivities, passing numerous vendors who were all selling the same selection of food. What I liked most about the walk was the lack of hard selling; I was asked a few times to make a purchase, but they didn't force their wares upon me. This gave me the impetus to refuse, but still continue winding my way onward, deeper into their lair.

Upon closer inspection the people serving were all dressed in the same company clothing. This may have been the reason I was being left alone; they were employees and not the owners of the stalls. Typically they wore a white long-sleeved top with a white apron which had thin red piping down the edges. The attire was topped off with either a hairnet, baseball cap or a wide-brimmed hat, with a coloured sash around the base. I think for their lower half they wore clothing of their own choice, as the items seemed to vary from person to person.

Even though I wasn't at all hungry, I still decided to get out of the midday sun, have a beer and sample a little of what they had to offer. I was leaving in a few hours, maybe never to return, so this would be my last chance; whatever I chose had to be better than my choice of breakfast. After ten minutes easing my way through the crowd I found a food outlet with a large seating area behind it. There I could sit at my own table, under a large communal awning and watch the festival unfold. When ordering I used my trusty finger to point towards the traditional plate of chiriuchu (cold dish) that had just been served to another customer.

This was to be washed down with a chilled bottle of Cusquena, which I had no concerns about whatsoever. Within a couple of minutes my selection was brought to the table and I cautiously lifted off the wedge of (what looked like) fish egg-covered bread to reveal the rest of the contents below. There I discovered a piece of chicken breast on the bone, some local cheese, lettuce, spicy pepper, a piece of a sausage, cancha (corn kernels) and of course the main attraction, a piece of cuy. The vermin was stuffed with a pungent smelling (and tasting) vegetable so it was once again difficult to describe the taste of the meat. While I wouldn't disagree with the people who venture that it is savoury, a little greasy and tastes like pork, it still isn't similar enough for me to be in total agreement.

I did sample all the items, but with very little enthusiasm. I had eaten too late this morning, but if I was hungry I am not sure I would have chosen guinea pig to fulfil my needs. Even though I am a traditionalist, there are some things that deserve to be preserved for posterity and some that don't. The consumption of rodents falls very much into the latter category for me; alternatives are available and they are better. It was good to be out of the sun though and the beer was just perfect.

To amuse me, I'm sure, an 'electrician' started working above my table, adding lights to the inside of the awning; it seemed the festivities were to continue into the night. As a qualified electrician I took more than a passing interest in his technique, as well as the task being undertaken. He began by stripping off some of the outer cable insulation with a pair of rusty pliers, which really isn't the best tool to use. He seemed oblivious to the fact that, while stripping the insulation off, he was firing offcuts into people's food. I think he was also working on the circuit while it was live because he was concentrating so hard on not touching the bare cables with his hand. He finally connected the prepared cable ends by carefully twisting them together with the insulated pliers and loosely covering with tape. I wished I could have stayed for the evening switch-on – I could have helped them put out the fire.

As I was contemplating what to do next a local woman caught my attention. She was wandering from table to table attempting to sell toilet rolls, which I thought was quite enterprising of her as there were no napkins to be found. The regular attendees would have no doubt brought something to wipe their hands on after eating with their fingers, so it was probably the tourists that were being targeted. The toilets were a good source of tissue paper for this need and no doubt well stocked, unless of course that was where she obtained her supply from! As she headed in my general direction and made eye contact I politely and rather lazily waved her away, but of course she ignored my gesture. I could have guessed that was going to happen – I always seem to attract people like her.

When she reached my table I once again made it obvious I was not going to make a purchase. Accepting defeat graciously, she then turned her attention to my food. While holding open an empty plastic bag she gestured towards my plate. As I wasn't particularly hungry I gave her the chicken and almost as an afterthought, the cuy. Thinking back, I don't know what possessed me to almost keep hold of the rodent. I suppose my first instinct was to give her something palatable to eat and not some half-chewed vermin.

Not content with my offering, though, the woman then picked up my paper plate and emptied the remainder of the contents into her bag and walked off! I was too stunned to respond, but then again if I was hungry, would I really have wanted to retrieve my lunch from the bottom of her smelly bag? A local woman sitting at an adjacent table had observed the exchange and had a look of genuine disbelief on her face. We couldn't speak each other's language, but words were unnecessary on this occasion; I just shrugged my shoulders and laughed. It was just as well she hadn't been thirsty because if she had tried that on with my beer then there would have been a fight! At 12:30 I paid the S/.32 bill and went for another walk.

I soon passed under a large banner – '*Bienvenidos al Festival del Chiriuchu*' (Welcome to the Festival of Chiriuchu) – and entered another large square. There I found balloon sellers and people sporting harnesses which held small advertising signs above their heads. This was a variation on the sandwich board idea, but these signs were a better design because they were elevated above the crowds. To keep them fully employed some also sold beers from a front pouch, which was nice to see.

The stalls now contained tourist-type bric-a-brac, DVDs and interesting, but cheap-looking, handmade items. Where there were no stalls the locals spread blankets on the floor and laid out their trinkets for sale, leaving very little space unused. I spent an hour just wandering around, taking in the atmosphere which was certainly much livelier than my previous visits around Cusco. The Peruvians certainly know how to throw a party; rather surprisingly though, there was very little in the way of religious overtones. This was just a case of eat, drink and be merry.

At 14:00 I headed back to the hotel to pick up my luggage and arrange for a taxi to take me to the airport.

Fortunately there was a taxi rank outside so I didn't have to wait at all, although I wouldn't have minded 'enduring' the air conditioning in the hotel lobby for a few minutes longer than I did. The journey itself only took twenty minutes; I hadn't realised the airport was so near. This made my coach journey now seem even worse, if that was possible.

Check-in was straightforward, as there was no queue at all for the desk, and they didn't even pass comment about my 26kg bag; my laptop I kept with me as hand luggage. After queuing at passport control for ten minutes, I then breezed right through the security scanner check as well; all these processes felt suspiciously too easy. At the departure lounge I learned there was a fifty-minute delay to the flight, which brought some normality to proceedings. I had been pre-warned by the hikers that this was a common occurrence at this time of day; I am not sure how they were so well informed.

I was advised to wait at gate four, but as the flight was delayed this would be subject to change. Rather frustratingly all the PA announcements were in Spanish only, so it was going to prove a little difficult for me to keep track of any alterations.

After fifteen minutes I spotted a Peruvian Airways rep loitering between gates three and four and approached her for news about the flight. All I learned was that she too was heading for Lima, so I would have to wait for the displays to indicate the correct gate. I found myself spending the next thirty minutes watching her like a hawk.

Of course 'the powers that be' did change the gate number, which would have been OK if the rep hadn't suddenly disappeared. I had only glanced up at the departure board for a moment, but as soon as I looked back she was gone. My flight had also been removed from the display on gate four. Although announcements were being made, I had no way of knowing if they related to my flight. I sat for a moment, watching the people around me as they all rose in unison to head to another location. As it was crowded, it was hard to determine their final destination, but with little other choice I decided to follow them. As I neared the desk at gate three I thankfully saw my absentee rep sitting behind the counter, oblivious of the angst she had just caused me.

My winged chariot arrived a further ten minutes later than scheduled, rounding up the delay to the full hour. Given the short flight time, it was surprising that this is such a common issue. Surely they could have identified the cause and addressed it? I wasn't overly concerned with the time it was taking, it was just frustrating not knowing where and when I was to board. As the announcements were incomprehensible to me I could have quite easily missed the flight altogether.

We landed just before 18:00 and I caught the shuttle bus to the terminal in a couple of minutes. I then looked out for passport control, before remembering I was on a domestic flight. The luggage carousels were sited conveniently in front of the arrival doors, adjacent to a very large Inca Kola sign. It took ten minutes for my luggage to appear, but at no time did I have to fight the urge to dash off and buy a bottle of that delicious, illuminous yellow beverage.

Upon entering the arrivals hall, I passed a very long queue at the taxi booking desk. When arranging my flight I hadn't thought to book a taxi to the hotel; this now looked like a big mistake. In desperation I headed outside to look for a taxi rank, but there simply wasn't any provision other than the booking desk. So back I went to join the queue and take my medicine. The problem with airport taxi runs is that they are invariably time consuming; some drivers may take well over an hour, due to traffic and distance, to make a round trip. As they only have a finite group of drivers the waiting time gets longer the further back you are in the queue.

Once I had prepaid for my journey I then had to wait for my driver to make an appearance. This is an example of why I normally plan everything well in advance; when I try to make these last-minute ad-hoc arrangements I always seem to forget to do something. An hour after landing I set off to the hotel, relieved to finally be on my way. Fortunately the traffic wasn't too bad and we arrived at my new accommodation at 19:30. I then discovered to my horror that I had managed to book a hotel without a bar! Five and a half hours travelling and no refreshments to greet me at the end of my journey…not even a Pisco sour!

As the Wi-Fi in my room was not connecting properly I had to trust to my map to find a place known as 'Pizza Street'. This was not its real name of course, but how it was often referred to by the locals, or so I thought. I understood that the street was full of restaurants and bars frequented by tourists and locals alike; during my pre-trip research I had chanced upon some reviews which suggested it was worth a visit.

After fifteen minutes walking in the general direction, twisting and turning through side roads, I had to admit to myself I was lost. It was getting dark now and I found it very difficult to read the street signs to confirm my bearings. With no one to ask I wandered on until I managed to accost a taxi driver at some traffic lights. I thought that was the end of my problems, but that proved not to be the case. His English was as good as my Spanish and he had never heard of Pizza Street.

I tried my best to describe a place I had never been to, relying on my memory of the photos from the internet, but there are only so many times you can say "pizza". I really should have written down the proper name of the street, but I had left my room in a hurry. To add to my frustration, he couldn't read my small map while he was driving and the traffic behind us prevented us from immediately pulling over. Eventually we did manage to turn into a quiet road where we regrouped; I was relieved to find that 'Calle de las Pizzas' was only a five-minute drive away. The fare only cost S/.5, so I gave him S/.10 for his trouble; he had been very helpful for very little money.

Before me lay a one-hundred-metre pedestrianised street, lined on both sides with mainly restaurants, but there were also some bars/clubs. This was the kind of area I had been looking for when I first arrived in Miraflores.

When I reached the end of the street and had viewed all of the premises I turned back and selected the busiest of the restaurants – there was an obvious choice as it was very lively. From the menu I chose 'Jalea Mixta', a dish of mixed fish, octopus and squid – all in batter served with some chips. This was not the healthiest of meals, but I reasoned it was good beer food. Instead of Cusquena I selected a bottle of Pilsner for a change, which proved to be a good selection.

Los Incas was larger than most of the restaurants I had visited in Lima. There were a few steps leading from the ground floor to a slightly elevated upper level, which must have annoyed the waitresses as it appeared to serve no real purpose. It was nice to see Inca traditions alive and well in Lima. All the furniture was made of dark wood and the tables had fabric coverings on them that were unmistakably of Peruvian design with their multitude of colours.

The clientele were a mixture of groups of young Peruvians and tourist couples. There was a buzz of conversation in the air and people were enjoying themselves. This felt like the sort of place back home where friends would meet straight from work, a place where people could chill out after their hard working week. The waitresses on the other hand looked stressed as they quickly moved between tables, either taking orders or delivering them. I don't envy people who work in restaurants and bars; it's a thankless task serving the public, especially when they are drunk. I have tried it for myself in my younger days, while undertaking my electrical apprenticeship. My friend got me a job working weekend and evening shifts in a local pub, never again.

The plate of food I received was huge, which meant I could pick the best parts, leave others and still have my fill. The generous portions must have been the reason for the restaurant being so popular. After a while though, I got fed up with the greasy batter taste and the thin layer of oil on my lips was making my beer go flat. After eating I left and headed back to the hotel; of course I got lost again and had to catch another taxi. Hopefully tomorrow when I returned I would have better luck; my new hotel would be a lot closer and hopefully I wouldn't be as tired.

CHAPTER SIXTEEN

Lima

I awoke to a free morning, after having sensibly chosen to fly to Lima yesterday afternoon. What I really needed now was some ideas on how best to use the time. I knew I had to try the internet, but last night I had trouble even establishing a Wi-Fi connection. Hopefully I would fare better this morning…ever the optimist. After several attempts I still couldn't make it work so I abandoned the Wi-Fi option, removed the main data cable from my room's modem and plugged it directly into my laptop. Unbelievably (to me, anyway) it worked, so all I had to do now was search for something interesting to do until checkout time.

It didn't take me long to find Huaca Pucllana on a very short list of nearby places to visit. This was one of the sites I had viewed from the top of the tour bus during my first stay in Lima. The thing I most remember about it was that it didn't look very interesting or pleasing to the eye. It also pre-dated the Incas so it wasn't altogether in keeping with the theme of this trip. But as it was only a short walk from the hotel and I had nothing else to do, I thought I would take a closer look.

After only walking for fifteen minutes in the general direction of the site I turned into a side road and there it stood before me. Its appearance took me somewhat by surprise as I was just about to consult my map. The surrounding houses had shielded this sizeable structure from me until then. I had an aerial photo which showed that one half of the site was based on the top of a hill; the other was at street level. Overall the site covered an area measuring approximately two hundred and fifty metres by one hundred metres.

What wasn't clear from my map was where the entrance lay, so I now had a choice to go left or right. With no one to ask I opted to go left, as I had done with Caesar when I was lost in the orchard. As I walked alongside the perimeter I peered through the high railings at the pyramid section which seemed to be constructed from small, rectangular clay bricks. They were all the same size, uniform in colour and very dusty looking, as you would expect. The entire boundary of the site was ringed by trees, almost in an attempt to hide the site from view of the local residents. I wonder if this is the case, as it isn't the prettiest monument I have seen. Were they ashamed of it, was it considered an eyesore, despite its historic value?

After walking for five minutes I stopped a passer-by to confirm I was heading in the right direction. Rather annoyingly I was informed I was heading the wrong way, so I had to turn around and retrace my steps. Fortunately I was in no particular hurry this morning and the weather was quite pleasant.

It is amazing how often this type of thing happens to me. I often have an equal chance of being right, but I so often get it wrong. On this occasion I am fairly sure the mistake made no significant difference, but there must have been times when this type of decision did. How many old and new acquaintances do I inadvertently miss by choosing the wrong option? How many opportunities pass me by without my realising and taking advantage? Sometimes the misses caused by these mistakes are close so I am aware of them, like spotting people I know as a train pulls away, leaving them on the platform. On other occasions I learn of recent departures from a third party, hopefully not as a result of my imminent arrival! I like to think my life is orderly and I am in control of my own destiny, but really it is almost a random chain of events (within the overall structure of my day) that I am experiencing. When you look at life in fine detail there are so many variables – each day is always different from the last, even in some small way.

The entrance fee to Huaca Pucllana was a very reasonable S/.12 and included a guided tour. A large purple sign informed visitors that it was actually forbidden to enter the archaeological site without the guide and it was closed on Tuesdays. As I only had a couple of minutes to wait before the 10:00 tour it seemed my impromptu detour had not affected today's schedule at all. If I had indeed arrived a little earlier, I would only have just been sitting in the waiting area a little longer.

When the guide arrived we set off with four other people in tow, beginning the tour with a visit to the nearby museum. It wasn't a long visit as there was only one room and a small collection of exhibits, but I did learn about the history of the site. Despite being over one thousand years old it was only excavated by experts in 1981, before being made an historical and cultural park ten years later. Given its size I thought this was a remarkable fact, to leave such a large plot undeveloped for hundreds of years is even a little perplexing. I would imagine the elevated pyramid part would have looked challenging from a development point of view. But the lower part, containing what was thought to be the administrative area, considerably less so. Recent attempts at developing the area were thankfully halted, but not before some oaf had cut a road through the lower section, dividing it in two.

The site construction looked extremely primitive, a little too primitive to have been built by the Incas. There were no stone walls here, just rows and rows of pre-formed clay bricks. The builders had used the site as a temple and a place to govern the people, while later inhabitants used the site for sacrifices and burials.

On one side of the room I came upon large pots decorated with pictures of animals, while glass display cases contained the smaller relics. But of all the items on display, the most relevant item was probably a reconstructed piece of wall. This allowed for a close-up view of the construction method, which was a significant part of the whole build. The clay bricks in this example were approximately 200mm x 150mm x 50mm in size and stacked vertically, five rows high, with horizontal clay mortar separating each row. As they were all butted together they looked like books on a library shelf.

After leaving the museum we passed a large restaurant and headed into the lower section of the site. This area was roped off in places, providing us with a designated walking route; occasionally the ropes were supplemented by wooden bridges. The excavated sections were divided by thousands of the clay bricks; some of these areas contained small rooms or complete roofless buildings.

To help tourists imagine what life would have been like, there were life-sized, scantily clad clay figures in some of the pits. The characters were in various action poses – some were toiling over the earth, others lifting pots or preparing a fire. They were smaller in height than the average European, but very stocky and heavy set; in fact they were not unlike the modern-day Peruvians I had seen in Cusco and the surrounding areas.

The next section housed live examples of the type of animal they kept to sustain themselves; both cuy and llamas featured, unsurprisingly. The fossilised remains of these animals (as well as fish) had been found in the neighbouring pits. As some of the skeletons were whole it led to the conclusion that they were sacrificed to the gods, rather than eaten, which seemed a waste of good food. It seemed a little unnecessary to incorporate a small zoo in this extremely dusty environment. If clay representations were made of the men, could they not have done something similar with the animals?

For the last part of the tour I now had to drag myself up to the top of the pyramid. It was a steep climb up the purpose-built, dusty, earthen ramp. When visiting, I would suggest wearing clothes that were destined for the washing pile upon the return to the hotel. At the top we had a good view of the whole site and the surrounding high-rise residential blocks of modern-day Lima, which was quite a contrast.

The main attraction at the top of the pyramid was a small Wari tomb built into one of the walls. The tomb contained the bones of both a priest and a fisherman as well as the remains of several sacrificed children. Some personal belongings were also placed around the bodies, something for them to use in the afterlife. The guide told us that the Wari Indians pre-dated the Incas by several hundred years, but drought and famine brought an end to their reign. This may have influenced the Incas and led them to develop aqueducts and bulk storage facilities.

The tour came to an end after an hour and although it was interesting in places, it was also a little underwhelming if I am being honest. To be fair though, it is an archaeological dig and not a grand palace; when thought of in those terms it does not disappoint. I thanked the guide for her time and the knowledge she conveyed, gave a tip of S/.20 and departed.

As I walked back to the hotel my calf muscles began to seize up; the last few days had really taken their toll on my legs. I was almost hobbling along when I made it back to the hotel. I think the walk up to the top of the pyramid had been one mountain too many for my weary limbs. With only half an hour left before checkout time I visited the hotel massage suite and explained the problem. I asked the masseur to concentrate on my legs only, given my limited time and needs. This turned out to be one of the best decisions I made during this trip. It didn't take long before I was advised that my legs were full of lactic acid. The masseur worked hard on my calves and when finished told me to go for a short walk, followed by a cold shower. I did as he suggested and it worked perfectly; the transformation was astounding – I was back to normal within minutes of getting dressed.

I checked out at midday and took a taxi to the Radisson hotel, arriving in just fifteen minutes. At the check-in desk I was advised that my room would not be ready until 15:00. The concierge helpfully added that if a room became available any quicker he would let me know. I was not completely convinced that I would be contacted, but just in case I left word that I may be reached on the second floor, where I would be having lunch in the main restaurant.

They must have just opened as I had the place to myself when I arrived. Before I was even seated my gaze immediately fell upon the central island that was populated with fancily prepared cold starters. For a set price I could have my fill, before also ordering some hot food from the menu. I chose not to overindulge, but there were a lot of tempting items on display.

After one or two passes of the table I selected a shot glass of prawn cocktail, a similar lobster-meat cocktail served on a Chinese soup spoon, some sushi and some salad. I could have had a lot more, but this was only the beginning. From the menu I chose chicken in black bean sauce and boiled rice. I finished off with a visit to the dessert table where I chose a chocolate mousse and a cheese cake. It may sound a lot of food, but the buffet portions were all bitesize in general.

Lunch had a decidedly East Asian feel to it, with a little Peruvian twist thrown in, a fusion of the two perhaps. During the meal the porter approached me and presented me with a card to my room. I was informed that I had been upgraded as I had booked for two nights. It seemed that it wasn't only the restaurant that was empty. There are cheaper hotels to stay in, but during the planning stage I had thought I might be in need of some pampering. I really had no way of knowing just how much the horse riding and trek were going to affect me. I was in my room by 13:30, where I rested up for an hour.

This evening I planned to return to Pizza Street for some drinks and my evening meal. I had selected this particular hotel because it was on a main road which led directly to the beginning of the pedestrianised street, ensuring I could come and go without a map or getting lost. All the same I decided to stretch my refurbished legs and go on a recce; it would be even easier to find in the daylight. I found it after fifteen minutes with no trouble at all, so it seemed the taxi drivers would go hungry tonight. It was really quiet at this time of day and as I had already eaten, and my mission complete, I took a slow walk back to the hotel.

After a good afternoons rest I left my room and headed for the hotel bar. As well as an upgrade I had also been given a $10.00 drinks voucher to use at the hotel bar for each night of my stay. I put it to good use by ordering a large gin and tonic before heading out for the evening. I arrived at Pizza Street at 20:00 and it was a lot livelier than during my afternoon sortie. I headed straight for the English bar at the end of the street. I don't usually go to these sorts of places; I much prefer to try the local establishments, but the only other alternatives were restaurants or clubs.

It didn't take long before I saw a fight between an Englishman and a Peruvian, two big men who were old enough to know better. I didn't see the start of it, but the Englishman was the one most aggrieved and was taken outside by friends to cool off. The Peruvian remained and just sat at the bar shaking his head, leading me to believe it was the Englishman who was at fault.

After a few drinks I adjourned to the same restaurant I had visited the previous night, but this time I chose 'Pescado a la Plancha', which translates as grilled fish, salad and chips. It was very busy again, but I had no trouble finding myself a table. I wouldn't describe this place as fine dining, but the prices are reasonable, the portions large and there was a good atmosphere.

I had a fairly quiet and relaxing day today, but tomorrow I was in for some real excitement. I had booked an excursion to fly over the Nazca Lines in a really small aeroplane and I don't particularly like flying. Many years ago I had attempted to rid myself of my fear of heights (and flying) by parachuting out of a tiny Cessna aircraft. I was twenty-four years old at the time and I quite often had stupid ideas like that. I reasoned that if I could jump out of a small aircraft, at fifteen hundred metres, then I would feel more comfortable sitting safely inside a very large passenger liner. It hadn't worked; in fact, it actually made things worse.

After overcoming my initial anxiety, I found the jump to be a most exhilarating experience. My impulsive nature had helped me exit the craft, despite a slight hesitation and a verbal prompt from the instructor. Once the noise of the aeroplane engine faded, I found inner peace in the silence. Using the toggles, I steered my way to the landing area and executed the landing perfectly, which is code for 'without injury'.

The fact I undertook a second jump four years later was even more surprising, especially to me, given I had sworn I would never do it again. But by then I was a mature and wise twenty-eight-year-old who loved to organise events. I took eleven other simpletons from work with me; I really should have kept quiet when it was suggested, but sometimes I have difficulty saying "no".

This second jump did not pass without incident. I was in the lead group (of our three teams) and our turn was delayed until the ambulance left the landing zone. Someone from another group had landed badly and twisted their knee. Nothing too serious then, but the delay didn't help my nerves. Once on board I was sited at the back right-hand side, which meant I would be the last out and not the first as I was before. Not a big deal, but it meant I would watch the others go first and have to spend a little more time on board. When my turn arrived, the same instructor from my first jump uttered the same words to me as he had four years earlier:

"Are you going to jump?"

He must have thought I was hesitating, but I didn't feel that was the case, at least not this time round. I was in a seated position with my legs dangling out the door attempting to ensure I had a good handhold. I was desperate to launch myself out and form the star shape I had been trained to do. Previously I had sort of slipped out and tumbled uncontrollably until the parachute opened and righted me. On this occasion I executed the routine perfectly. Being in the right position enabled me to look up and see the parachute unfurl from a small ball to its full size, which was incredible to witness.

Unfortunately, the tug on the static line, which breaks the connection to the plane, dislodged something in my right shoulder. Although I felt no pain, maybe a slight ache, something was wrong. I later had some physio, but it was never repaired. I would describe the issue as a lazy shoulder; it now sits slightly lower than my left. I can move it into its correct position with no trouble and I have not experienced any pain whatsoever, but it is not right. I must have bent a bone without actually breaking it in my attempt to lock myself into the correct shape.

I landed perfectly and just in time to watch one of my colleagues getting dragged backwards through a hedge when the wind caught his grounded chute. Another was struggling with the controls and she was left (quite hilariously) heading for the motorway, some way off in the distance. A four-by-four was dispatched to chase after her; it was gone for some time as she was very light.

When I try to rationalise my fear of flying I think it comes down to one simple point…my brain cannot cope with a no-win situation. If I am on board an aircraft that gets into trouble I am not in the position to influence the outcome; as an engineer this is an alien concept for me. Hopefully for my flight over the Nazca Lines I wouldn't need a parachute, although I suspect we would be too close to the ground to make use of it in any case.

CHAPTER SEVENTEEN

Nazca Lines

I awoke early and in very good spirits until I remembered what lay in store for me today. I wasn't looking forward to this Nazca Lines outing at all, despite my interest in seeing these ancient drawings first hand. The thought of flying in a light aeroplane over a strange desert made me more than a little anxious.

Having read articles about the very poor safety records did little to ease my concerns. It seemed things had come to a head after a crash in 2010, which at the time of writing was only six years prior to my flight. [14] All aircraft were grounded and, of the forty-eight inspected, only seven were deemed fit for service. This prompted the government to introduce new legislation, relating mostly to servicing and repair, but also insisting on the use of a co-pilot. This was not really the sort of thing that I had wanted to learn, but I tried to take the positives – at least they were now attempting to address the problems.

While searching for alternatives to flying, I discovered that some of the lines may be viewed from the side of a mountain and there is also a viewing tower on a highway that cuts across the desert. I quickly dismissed these options because it seemed a waste of time to go that far just to see two or three examples. Today's flight was itself limited to viewing only thirteen of the geoglyphs from the hundreds of lines, geometric shapes, animals and plants available. This was somewhat regrettable, but the best that I could do.

At 06:30 I was picked up by my driver, Juan and we set off south along the coastal road, heading for the town of Pisco. Flying from Nazca itself would have put six hours onto my already long day as it was further away from Lima. A shorter drive of course meant a longer flight, which although not desirable, was the most practical approach. As it was still early and a Saturday, there was very little traffic on the roads, which made for a pleasant change.

The morning sky was cloudy, white and overcast, so at this stage I wondered if the weather would prompt a cancellation. I wouldn't have minded that at all, something out of my control where I could just shrug my shoulders and reason that it just wasn't meant to be. Maybe as an alternative Juan would take some money to drive to the tower to view from there after all.

After just over an hour we stopped at a service station for coffee and a toasted sandwich, which was most welcome. I hadn't felt like eating when I was at the hotel, but now I was a little peckish. After a twenty-minute break we continued on our way, only to be hampered for several kilometres by what appeared to be some sort of cycling endurance race. Some of the cyclists even had slow-moving support cars behind them which effectively reduced the now busy dual carriageway down to one lane. I was beginning to get concerned about the time, which was ironic given that this might be the opportunity to abort the trip I was half hoping for.

The lines were formed by the local inhabitants of Nazca (a pre-Inca civilisation) who created the designs simply by clearing away the rocks and other debris. They no doubt would have used some sort of scaled drawing and some pegs to mark out the designs. The resulting clean spaces are what we see today; why they went to the trouble is still unknown so we can only speculate.

As the lines are very large, it is believed they were only intended to be viewed from high above. This of course has led people to believe that they were gifts to the gods, while those that believe in alien visitations are adamant that the intended recipients are from another world. Whatever the reason, they have survived for a thousand years, mainly due to the unusually dry and windless climate; although as late as 2009, rain did cause some damage (global warming?). The resulting silt that washed over them had to be painstakingly removed by experts to restore them to their former glory.

We arrived at the airport at 10:00, at which point Juan changed hats and became my tour administrator. From the carpark I was led into a small reception area where documents were being checked by airport officials. I had remembered to bring my passport and electronic voucher so there were no last-minute dramas with paperwork. But before I could enter the departure lounge I had to attend another desk to pay S/.12 airport tax, which seemed a bit unnecessary. The price must fluctuate, I can think of no other reason why it wasn't automatically added to the cost of my tour. Once I was booked in, Juan returned to the car where he would await my return.

Within the departure lounge there were three separate groups of people, all Japanese, if I was not mistaken. I had just over half an hour remaining before my 11:00 take-off. I spent my time constructively looking out of the window praying for the weather to worsen. Unfortunately, we had left the bad weather behind us in Lima; the sky had now cleared to a light blue expanse as far as the eye could see. It seemed that Mother Nature was not going to come to my rescue today; the shaman's work no doubt.

At the allotted time there was a call for my group to step forward towards the departure lounge outer door. We were then led outside and told to follow the designated route, staying as close to the main building as possible. As we neared our craft we were then allowed to cross the open space and form an orderly queue at the door. Post-trip I learned that the aeroplane was a twelve-seater Cessna 208b Caravan 1 (designation OB-2001P) built in 2011. It would have been reassuring to know, prior to boarding, that it was a fairly new craft and not one involved in the previous failures.

I had eleven Japanese tourists for company (mostly women) and they all seemed relaxed enough, at least I could see no anxiety or fear in their eyes. Once on board I found the seats were all singles, one row to each side, with a central aisle to pass through. I was allocated seat number three on the left, near the front, so I had just one passenger directly in front of me and the two pilots at the very front. From my position I could clearly see the instrument dials, so I would be able to keep one eye on our altitude.

The flight was scheduled to take ninety minutes, which was a long time to keep my mind occupied. For the first twenty minutes we flew at seven hundred and fifty metres, before ascending to a lofty three thousand metres. I thought the pilot was climbing to provide us with a better view of the drawings. But as the co-pilot announced we were nearing the site we dropped back down to our original altitude, making the reason for the climb a mystery.

Once in final approach position the co-pilot turned around and calmly announced, over the noise of the engine, that we would soon see the 'Whale' on the left-hand side. I readied my camera and scanned the desert floor for signs of anything that resembled a whale; I knew this would take split-second timing if I was to capture decent photos. Although given my vantage point, I was beginning to have my doubts if I was going to see anything of note at all. We were up so high, so far away from the desert floor, a floor that was hardly devoid of marks – there seemed to be lines everywhere. I just had to hope I could distinguish between the intended and unintended markings.

Without warning, the pilot sharply dropped the left wing and we plummeted towards the ground. The engine screamed in protest, whining and droning in that wartime dive-bombing sort of way. I was half expecting to hear a strafe of bullets strike the ground. There was a collective gasp from most of the passengers on board and my heart missed several beats. In mid-dive the co-pilot was enthusiastically thrusting his right hand back and forth gesturing towards an unknown (to me) space on the ground. I, for my part, tried desperately to hang on to something, anything to regain my upright seating position, while at the same time attempting to gather my wits. Needless to say, I didn't even see the 'Whale', let alone take a photo.

After what felt like ten seconds we levelled off again and began to steadily climb back to our original altitude. The aeroplane's fuel thankfully returned to the engine, the blood to my heart. Right on cue the Japanese all began to clap with uniform excitement; they were actually enjoying this life-threatening experience! (Here I was going to make a joke about Japanese and kamikaze, but then I thought it might be in poor taste). It felt like I was in a horror film or locked away in a mental asylum, while being the only sane person left in the world. This was utter madness and to think I had earlier been worried in case there was a little turbulence!

As the passengers on the right-hand side now had to be accommodated we slowly turned and began another approach, this time from the opposite direction. It was then I realised that there weren't to be thirteen suicidal plunges towards the earth, but twice that number. At least I was more prepared on this occasion, even if I only saw blue sky from my window.

Even though I desperately wanted to capture all of the drawings on camera, I somehow missed a few altogether. Given their size, this is an extraordinary admission to

make and one I am struggling to explain. It was extremely difficult to persuade my brain to scan an area while at the same time ignoring the ground that was zooming ever closer. The ones I tried to view, but missed, were:
Ballena – Whale (understandably)
Condor – Condor
Alcatraz – Heron bird (but got a photo, somehow)

On more than one occasion the pilot, not content with merely flying the plane, decided to assist his colleague with the identification of the drawings. This was more than a little disconcerting as I then had two lunatics facing me, both now pointing in my general direction with no one at the controls. I now knew why a co-pilot had been assigned to each trip; it seemed incomprehensible that this was only a recent addition. But this safety precaution really is negated when the pilot reverts back to his old ways. At these times I found it difficult to look out the window and trust my fortunes to this reckless pair. While they were 'helping' the passengers I felt almost compelled to look after the plane, ready to offer the pilot advice on our position when the time came.

In one of my aerial photos I did unexpectedly capture the viewing tower alongside a road. I now know it is sited very close to the 'Tree' and the 'Hands', which sit together side by side. Although they are clearly within a few metres of the tower it still doesn't appear high enough to fully appreciate them. However, I now wish I had made an effort to arrange a visit, because it might have been interesting to view them from another perspective.

Despite my initial issues with the flight I did, however, manage to view the following, but only captured the ones marked with a (photo) for posterity:

Compass – Compass
Trapezoides – Trapezoids (photo)
Astronauta – Astronaut (photo)
Mono – Monkey (photo)
Perro – Dog
Calibri – Humming Bird (photo)
Arana – Spider
Lorro – Parrot (photo)
Manos – Hands (photo)
Arbol – Tree (photo)

Halfway through the flight I began to feel a little nauseous with all the diving and climbing, but I found (when I was able) that focussing on the horizon helped. I also felt a little light-headed on the way back to the airport, but thankfully there was no turbulence to speak of and the acrobatics were well and truly behind us. The return journey passed really quickly and it wasn't long before we were back on the ground. With the assistance of a fellow passenger I had some photos taken of me in front of the aircraft, before giving a quiet blessing to the ground I walked on.

My concerns over the flight had proved to be justified; the experience will live with me for some considerable time. The pilots must get a buzz out of terrifying their passengers, but I don't share their enthusiasm. There is a balance to be struck between risk and reward and this tipped towards the risk side of the equation a little too far for my liking. I felt it would have been a stupid way to die, just to see some lines in a desert drawn by primitive Indians.

It terms of artistic design I thought the lines were a bit of a mixed bag. Dogs don't have all four legs on the same side of their bodies; the Whale (I have seen pictures of) is almost indistinguishable from a fish or indeed most other sea creatures. The Astronaut is the one that the alien conspiracy theorists have latched onto the most, as they insist that the oval head is in fact a space helmet, hence the name. Given what I have stated about the Dog and the Whale, isn't it more likely that it was simply a poor drawing? Conversely there are some that are truly remarkable – I have seen good pictures of the Spider, the Tree, the Condor, the Heron bird and the Hummingbird and they must have been drawn by another team. The detail seems to have been captured perfectly from the source material, maybe not always anatomically correct, but certainly artistically with merit.

If some good has come of this experience then it is the discovery that I am now not as worried about turbulence as I once was, although my fear of flying overall still remains alive and well. The problem is I still have a logical mind, the mind of an engineer, and the reports concerning poor or little maintenance of these aeroplanes are what I have long suspected. I have worked with and managed a number of engineers who have grown complacent over the years. 'That'll do' is their mantra because things seldom go wrong, but that attitude really 'won't do' when it comes to aeroplane maintenance.

We were back on the road just before 13:00 and as we drove Juan offered me a choice of where to stop for lunch. It was either to be in the vicinity of the airport, which looked a bit drab, or a little place he knew along the way. I went with his recommendation and after an hour we stopped at a service station which initially took me by surprise. But I soon discovered my concerns were misplaced, as the large restaurant was very busy, unusually so for this type of drive-through venue. It was no doubt swelled by groups of people watching the Champions League final between Real Madrid and Atletico Madrid, but even so it must have built quite a reputation to attract the people here in the first place.

Juan selected what looked like a Peruvian type of sushi, which seemed to be the speciality of the house, judging by the signs over the bar. On his plate were three California rolls, but instead of rice on the outside it looked more like polenta. Inside looked like cucumber and atop each were medleys of different seafood items, each with an artistic sweep of sauce in front. I ordered trout with a seafood medley on top, which was accompanied by mashed potato swirls, asparagus and an orange sauce. Each dish was well presented and several levels above what I had initially expected from a service station restaurant. After a leisurely hour we were ready to leave, so I paid the bill which came to a reasonable S/.81 for both of our meals, rounding up to S/.100 to include a tip.

The return journey to the hotel was uneventful; there was the expected traffic, but we kept to a steady pace, arriving back at 17:30. I gave Juan a tip of S/.50, which I think surprised him as I had also paid for his lunch. After he departed I headed straight to the bar adjacent to reception for a stiff drink. It was still a little quiet, so I just had the one large gin and tonic before returning to my room.

For my evening meal I ventured out to an Indian restaurant, as I am a big fan of the cuisine. It only cost S/.15 by taxi and despite the driver being unfamiliar with the area we found the restaurant straight away, to both our surprises. It was 19:00 when I arrived and the place was a little short of customers – I should have taken that as a sign. For the starter I chose some fish, as it would be lighter and easier to digest than chicken or lamb and for a main course I chose my default dish of chicken madras.

When the fish arrived I found it to be very dry due to the fine breadcrumb coating and it had little in the way of taste; the accompanying dips were fine, but I have had better. I had hoped that the main course would rescue the meal, but that wasn't to be the case. I know a madras curry contains mustard seeds, but I don't usually see them floating around in such a pale sauce. Everything was wrong, from the colour, to the taste, to the mild flavour. The chef clearly had no experience of making the dish. I should really have sent it back, but I had lost my appetite and they spoke little English. I ate a little more than I should have; I guess I was trying to persuade myself it was OK when it really wasn't. The bill came to S/.118, which I paid without leaving a tip, putting this one down to experience.

There was a taxi parked outside which I took back to the hotel. After another large gin and tonic at the bar, which proved to be the highlight of the evening, I retired to my room. I had intended to go out for one last hurrah tonight, but as I had eaten (to a degree) and didn't fancy any more to drink I didn't bother. I was winding down now and the last thing I needed tomorrow was a hangover on my very long flight home.

CHAPTER EIGHTEEN

Last Day

Had it really only been eighteen days? It certainly felt much longer, probably because I had squeezed in a lot of amazing experiences. Whether I was riding over the mountains, trying new foods or simply taking in the scenery, it was all so different to my life back home. It was true there had been challenges, particularly towards the end, but that is all part of travelling abroad, into the unknown. But on this final day all that seemed behind me; my mind was now turning towards home. Living out of a suitcase loses its charm after a while, no matter how nice the surroundings are or how great a time is being experienced.

But before I headed for the airport I had one last place to visit – a mansion/museum called Casa de Aliaga. It felt fitting to leave this excursion until the end as it was built by the Spanish invaders. In 1535 Francisco Pizarro presented the site, where the mansion was to be built, to a friend and officer called Jerónimo de Aliaga as a reward for his assistance during the Inca conquest. His descendants have lived there ever since, ensuring the buildings preservation from generation to generation. Many refurbishments have taken place, but it is believed to be the oldest residence in the whole of the Americas.

At 10:00 I checked out of the hotel, leaving my luggage behind in a secure room. From the door I could see the receptionist balancing my laptop precariously on top of my large case. Instead of explaining the obvious, I entered the room and moved it to the floor. I had no trouble obtaining transport as the hotel had a taxi rank directly outside with a driver waiting; I didn't think to ask about the cost of the trip.

I had expected the twelve-kilometre drive across town to take about twenty to thirty minutes, but of course it wasn't going to be that easy. We were only two minutes into the journey when the driver received a phone call; I wasn't overly impressed when he answered. But it seems the natives of this country had yet to embrace the concept that using a mobile phone while driving somewhat impairs your concentration. I was even less impressed when he turned around and deposited me back outside the hotel. It seemed he had received a better offer! The decision had clearly been made so it wasn't even worth complaining; my protestations would have fallen on deaf ears. He hailed me a passing taxi, jumped back into his car and sped off.

My new driver took the dual carriageway as soon as he was able; this road not only bisected the city it also carved a near straight line towards my destination. As we neared my drop-off point we took the slip road and headed towards the old town main square. We were then waylaid by heavy traffic – today was Sunday and of course the peak of the Corpus Christi celebration; I hadn't considered that, until now. This may have been nice for the participants, but it wasn't so good for tourists with only a few hours of their trip left. After five minutes of attempted back doubles, I told him to stop and let me out. I thought the fare of S/.20 represented good value for the time and distance, not to mention his trouble.

Starting at the Plaza San Martin, I navigated my way through several streets towards the Plaza de Armas de Lima. Upon arrival I immediately recognised the square from my bus tour, two weeks earlier, although it now looked very different. There were thousands of people milling around, waiting for the ceremony to begin. As it looked impossible to navigate my way straight through the tightly bunched crowd, I stuck close to the buildings and took a more circular route around the perimeter. This allowed me some freedom of movement and I was also able to people watch as I walked. The main protagonists were priests all wearing blue two-piece robes; around their necks they all wore a thick, white, single knotted rope. They looked as if they were all attending a mass hanging. I suppose they were indeed human sacrifices of sorts, given their choice of lifestyle.

It was starting to get hot now and I was beginning to wish I had picked another day for this visit. I continued onward, using my experience to keep to the shadows formed by the shops; I could already feel the sun burning my skin. Once on the far side of the square I made enquiries as to the location of Casa de Aliaga; I had a map but the scale now made it of little use. I was directed to a pedestrianised street; halfway along I made further enquiries of a man standing in a doorway, only to discover he was a guide standing outside the very building I was looking for. In my defence the building didn't have a single sign to identify it, not even a door number.

The outer two-storey façade masked the size of the property, making it appear to be a small house rather than a mansion. The upper part of the front façade was constructed in one continuous piece of medium brown wood and contained lots of windows. Below, either side of the main entrance, were small independent shops, which rather spoiled the overall look in my opinion. I would have at least insisted the shops fitted in with the theme of the building frontage.

I didn't feel a private tour was really necessary as it was a medium-sized mansion rather than a grand palace, but I thought I might learn some interesting facts. After paying the S/.30 I entered through the small wooden entrance door where I was immediately faced with a marble staircase leading to the upper floor. As I trudged up the steps I noticed the orange walls on either side were patched up with white filler and when I reached the top I came upon a scaffold. It seemed they didn't close the museum for restoration works.

At the top and to my right was an ornate wooden lattice type doorway. It was framed by pillars four metres high, with decorative turned wooden dowels throughout. The upper part above the central doors formed what looked like a sun shape, with the dowels forming the rays emanating from its centre; carved inlays completed the piece. I continued along the central corridor and into the main part of the mansion.

I found the rooms very spacious and most contained large period portrait paintings everywhere I looked; I suppose after nearly five hundred years there were plenty of family members to exhibit. The floors were either tiled or completely covered in expensive looking carpets. The supporting cabinets, tables and chandeliers all blended in together, despite being acquired in different eras.

This was a time well before the use of plastics and vinyl, a time where quality handmade items were the norm for those that could afford them. It would have been interesting to see the section of the house closed off to the public, the spaces where the current owners resided. I would like to know if they had abandoned this retro style of furnishings and embraced more modern comforts.

At the heart of the structure there was even room for an inner courtyard, which added much-needed light to the rooms. The escorted tour ended with a visit to the chapel which was lined from floor to ceiling in wooden panels, completed by a small altar. Upon departing the chapel, I was left to wander through the rest of the rooms alone. In the main living room, *Salón de los Azulejos*, there was a painting of Señor Aliaga himself. It seemed mandatory in those days for the men to sport both a moustache and beard. In the far corner of the room there was a glass-fronted case containing the sword he used during the Inca conflict.

Once I had visited all of the rooms and seen all there was to see I made my way to the exit. This had been a most interesting place to visit, full of history. Given the grandeur it was hard to imagine people living there – it felt like a museum rather than a home.

I now headed away from the main square to avoid the crowds and after twenty minutes I found myself in China town. It would have been interesting to try some more Peruvian/Chinese fusion, but I wasn't at all hungry. This was rather fortunate as none of the restaurants looked very clean and welcoming. After my Indian experience I was now a little wary about non-Peruvian cuisine. After an hour or so wandering around I decided to head back to the familiarity of the hotel area. The last thing I needed at this stage was to get lost and have to rush around trying to find my way back to the hotel.

On one of the main roads I found a bus stop that listed the actual road my hotel was located on. When I say bus stop it takes a bit more explaining than that. The waiting area was located on an elevated platform, a metre up from the road, with a ticket machine adjacent to a turnstile gate. This arrangement was more in keeping with a metro/underground system. When purchasing my ticket, I discovered that despite this being the cross-city shuttle bus, it still only cost a few soles. When the bus arrived it lined up perfectly with the sliding glass doors on the platform and we all boarded. It was standing room only by the time I entered, but at least I was on my way.

We were soon on the dual carriageway, in a dedicated central lane for buses which made for an effortless journey. When my stop arrived I disembarked and inwardly congratulated myself on navigating the city so easily on my own. That was until I discovered that I was at the wrong end of the road; I then had to walk nearly two kilometres to the hotel. The best thing I could have done upon reaching the hotel was to have lunch. But as I had checked out I no longer felt like a guest, even though my luggage still resided in the property. Besides, I liked Pizza Street as there was so much variety and it wasn't that far away.

Upon arrival I chose to dine at a restaurant called Glorietta, mainly because no one pressurised me as I read the menu outside. Everywhere else someone was immediately on my shoulder as soon as I showed even the remotest interest in their establishment and that irritates me somewhat. Once seated, I perused the menu and chose some langoustines in a thick cheesy/fish sauce with some chips on the side. This I washed down with a small jug of sangria. Everything tasted OK, but this was not the last time I would think of this meal.

There was a three-piece band serenading the customers from just outside the restaurant. I felt like paying them to go away as I just considered them a nuisance. When they were finished they visited the tables hoping to be bestowed with money; some young lads thought it funny to remove the tip from their restaurant bill wallet and hand that over. I left just after 16:00 and took a very slow walk in the general direction of the hotel. I window-shopped as I walked, hoping the delay would eke away at the time, as I had allowed an hour to cover the fifteen-minute walking distance.

Although it was still early I preferred to wait at the airport instead of sitting around in the hotel reception. It was a very nice hotel, but the common areas were rather dark and less welcoming than they could have been. After retrieving my luggage I walked into the street to hail a taxi, ignoring the drivers waiting at the hotel rank. As expected, the traffic was horrendous, particularly as we neared the airport. I did feel a little sorry for the driver as he could have really done without an airport run at this time of day.

When I checked in at the departure desk I was advised that my British Airways Club World ticket came with access to a private lounge. I don't usually upgrade, but at the time of booking I had expected to be really tired after my Andes experience. It also had the added benefit of separating me from any noisy and misbehaving children. This was just as well, as it was now just after 19:00 and I was starting to feel a little unwell. There was quite a wide range of free food and drink in the lounge, but as I had no appetite at all, I just grabbed a bottle of water and sat in the quiet room.

At 21:00 I was on board, greeted by the cabin crew and presented with a glass of champagne. Ordinarily I would have welcomed an alcoholic drink, but on this occasion I could have done without it; I drank it anyway for my nerves. I had to turn down all the food I was offered though as my stomach was now doing somersaults. Early into the flight I made the first of several trips to the toilet. I had the worst case of diarrhoea I have ever had and was violently vomiting at the same time, filling the adjacent sink. If I had been at home I would have gone to hospital to have my stomach pumped. My choice of lunch venue had severely backfired. The flight took twelve hours and twenty minutes and I suffered through every minute.

Admittedly the last few days of my Peruvian adventure ended a little disappointingly with a car crash, hotel eviction and severe food poisoning. But, overall, I would describe the trip as a resounding success. I had ridden a wonderful horse over the Andes to Machu Picchu and, as a result, ticked another of the Seven Wonders of the World off my list.

The Mountain Lodges of Peru I would highly recommend, if you prefer a little comfort on your travels. The guides and staff were very friendly and did their best to accommodate my every wish, even if the occasional mistake was made. I am sure others would also endorse the Inca trail option for the experience and camaraderie. I can't imagine myself camping out in the wild, but if there were large campsites on the way with facilities, then it wouldn't be as bad as all that.

The Nazca Lines were also memorable, but I think that, given what I now know about the flight, it would be extremely unlikely that I would repeat the exercise. But, there is always the option to visit the tower and view a couple at eight to ten metres up. If I did select this option though, I would have to find something else to do in the immediate area as it is a long way from Lima.

I didn't have that much interaction with the modern-day Peruvians once I left the lodges. Once back in Cusco and Lima I trod the well-worn tourist path and mainly kept to myself. The Spanish influence is very evident, throughout the country, with language and religion major factors. Modern technology is also having an influence on the nation and it will eventually lead to the complete demise of the Inca heritage. It is easier to forget your ancestors when you are sitting in front of a television, eating meals bought from a supermarket or working in technological fields instead of the grass ones.

In terms of my itinerary I think I could have tackled it a little differently. I chose the route of:

- Flight from London to Lima
- Sightseeing in Lima
- Coach south, then east to Cusco (not recommended)
- Sightseeing in Cusco/Sacred Valley
- Riding along the Salkantay trail, staying in lodges
- Short flight from Cusco back to Lima
- Drive to Pisco for Nazca Lines flight
- Drive back to Lima
- Sightseeing in Lima
- Flight to London from Lima

I could have made life a little easier by allowing more time at the beginning and taking a more circular route:

- Flight from London to Lima
- Bus south to Nazca for the Nazca Lines flight
- Bus south to Lake Titicaca (overnight stay)
- Bus to Cusco (longer, but best bus route to Cusco)
- Sightseeing in Cusco/Sacred Valley
- Riding along the Salkantay trail, staying in lodges
- Short flight from Cusco back to Lima
- Sightseeing in Lima
- Flight to London from Lima

I hope you have enjoyed reading about my adventure and if you feel inspired to visit Peru yourself, there are some wonderful adventures to be had. As with all visits to foreign countries there are always one or two pitfalls, but I don't think any of the ones I experienced were intentional; the Peruvian people are simply too nice.

ONLINE SOURCES

1. https://library.brown.edu/create/modernlatinamerica/chapters/chapter-6-the-andes/moments-in-andean-history/chinese-peru/ Retrieved 25/02/18
2. https://www.chimuadventures.com/blog/2016/04/inca-kola-made-by-englishman/ Retrieved 06/07/18
3. https://www.rediscovermachupicchu.com/aqueducts.htm Retrieved 24/11/17
4. https://science.howstuffworks.com/innovation/inventions/5-ancient-incan-inventions4.htm Retrieved 19/11/17
5. http://www.discover-peru.org/inca-food/ Retrieved 26/11/17
6. https://www.aracari.com/inca-wheel/ Retrieved 26/11/17
7. http://www.discover-peru.org/inca-economy-society/ Retrieved 24/11/17
8. https://www.ancient.eu/Quipu/ Retrieved 20/11/17
9. https://ancientincareligion.weebly.com/rituals.html Retrieved 26/11/17
10. http://www.ancient-origins.net/history-famous-people/ Retrieved 26/11/17
11. https://en.wikipedia.org/wiki/Battle_of_Cajamarca Retrieved 26/11/17
12. https://howtoperu.com/weapons-and-armor-of-the-spanish-conquistadors/ Retrieved 20/11/17
13. https://www.thoughtco.com/biography-of-francisco-pizarro-2136558 Retrieved 26/11/17
14. https://www.worldnomads.com/travel-safety/south-america/peru/nasca-lines-of-peru-safety-tips-for-choosing-your-flight Retrieved 30/04/18

Lessons on a horse named Guinness

Peruvian potatoes

Alpaca Suri

Hotel El Mercado inner courtyard

Lunch

Salkantay Lodge

Humantay Lake

Up in the clouds

Wayra Lodge

One of the wider trails

Colpa Lodge

Cooked cuy

Lucma Lodge

Hiking the Inca trail

First view of Machu Picchu

The team on Huayna Picchu

Most recognisable part of Machu Picchu

Journey to the Sun Gate

Cessna 208b Caravan 1

The Humming Bird

* 9 7 8 1 7 8 4 5 6 5 9 8 5 *

ND - #0090 - 060826 - C278 - 197/132/18 - PB - 9781784565985 - Gloss Lamination